# OPEN YOUR EYES

*To A Clear Mind*

*Wise Actions and a Life of Grit*

L. CookHamilton

# Open Your Eyes

*To A Clear Mind*

*Wise Actions and a Life of Grit*

# Dedication

This book is respectfully and humbly dedicated to the proven invincibility of our African-American Ancestors.  To the life and memory of Mediba (Nelson Mandela). To my Granddaughter Hannah Hamilton.  As a sincere thank you to the many African American (A-A) parents who are working hard to support and parent their children into self-reliant and self-sustaining adults; and as inspirational, yet critical reading for those A-As who are self-destructing, feeding on themselves, engaging in poor-parenting, willingly contributing to our genocide, or walking unaware into slaughter.  And to those  of us who fail to realize that if our anger is misguided and internally destructive, we become a tool of the enemy who gleefully aids us in our self-destruction and the self-destruction of our communities.

# Thanks

Thanks to the Honorable Texas Congresswoman and later U.S. Congresswoman Barbara Jordan who allowed me to see a woman of color in command of the English language, speak with intelligence, eloquence, masterful diction, and courage. Back then, I was shocked to see with my own eyes such a woman of color.  I determined that although I grew up without have running water, indoor plumbing, wholly inadequate heating in the winter, a family food budget of $10.00 per week to feed 12 children; I too could dream and most importantly I could rise above my circumstances and pursue my dreams. Awesomely thanks to Dr. Dorothy Autrey, History Professor at Alabama State University, for helping me to appreciate the myriad of contributions and rich cultural heritage of the African American people primordially to present.  Thanks to Oprah Winfrey for encouraging me to live with purpose and intention. And thanks to President

Barack Obama and First Lady Michelle Obama for inspiring me with your examples of self-respect, immense dignity, mental prowess, strength of character, commitment to family; and as dedicated fulfillers of civic duty, motivated me to step forward with courage and conviction and write this book.    After reading this book, I am depending on you to step forward and use the information contained herein to help at least three others.  Each one teaches one…. Inaction is a slap in the face to our ancestors and our young… We can no longer stand by, analyze, complain, and make excuses.  Do something, say something, help with something…. Stop pontificating on how well you see the problem.  Become about action.   Less talk, more action.  Two ears, one mouth:  less talk more action.

## Individual Accountability

If you are favored by Universal Divine Forces to encounter this book, be mindful it is not a coincidence.  You should read it without delay. After having read it yourself, you are accountable to share the information with at least three others, especially young A-A men, and shortly thereafter, follow up with discussions to ensure the information has been understood and widely disseminated.  Each one teaches three.  We owe such a sincere dialogue to our invincible ancestors, to our youth, to the salvation of our culture, to the regeneration of our communities, and equally as important, we owe this truth to our humanity. We must open our own eyes, teach our own people to do the same, coalesce and begin to significantly increase self-sustaining efforts and positive causes in our lives and our communities.

## Of Note

There are time-tested books on religion and there is an ample supply of dedicated, capable and learned Clergy, Ministers, Monks, Priests, Rabbis, Imams, Teachers, Faith Leaders, and Religious Authorities to teach and help you pursue your faith of choice.  The Freedom of Religion is paramount to our rights as citizens.  I do not address  a certain group, branch, or denomination in this book, but I encourage you to embrace the Faith of your choice as a part of your life.

I have included many sidebars in this book in the form of text boxes.  Some are explained, while others are there to encourage you to do research if you desire to know about them.  Conducting your own research is intended to nudge you to become a life-long learner as an example to African-American youth.   Engaging in life-long study is essential to mental acuity and to maintaining the underlying mental prowess required to support wise decision discernment in everyday life.  Daily study, meditation, and some form of exercise, I opt for yoga, strength training,  and  walking, is  essential to a quality life balance.

# Contact Information

lincookhamilton@aol.com


**Website:** www.lcookhamilton.com

Facebook  @lindahamilton

Twitter @Lindacookhamilton

Instagram @lcookhamilton


334-368-2019

334-382-8893


# Ordering

https://www.amazon.com/dp/1733358226


Use contact information to arrange Speaking Engagements, Courses,

Training, and Life Coaching


x

# Table of Contents

page

# Preface

Our ancestral homeland, Africa, was a continent of great accomplishments including developed kingdoms and city states, infrastructures, universities (i.e. Timbuktu), mathematics such as fractal geometry, commerce, science, medicine (healers), language symbols, strong family traditions, cultural norms, and respect for environmental factors long before being invaded by Colonial Imperialists (CI); who willfully interrupted the "prime directive" or natural evolution that was underway.  Sometime after the Hunter Gather period ended and before the CI arrived on shore, the natural evolution had gone a bit awry and domestic slavery had seeped into the culture.  Since Cause and Effect or "what ye sow" is the underlying law in the Universe, it follows that, over eons, this negative practice of enslaving captures won in village to village or between tribal skirmishes

> *The Griots*
> Wandering human encyclopedias and custodians of African and African-American history.

would sow the seeds to attract more and more of this practice even from abroad.

Although the CI came to Africa under the banner of Christianity, their practice of enslavement would be eviler, wicked, sadistic, and one which would descend our African American ancestors into an extremely brutal, terroristic, wicked, and cruel

> **"Twenty Odd Negans"**
> **17 men and 3 Women**
>
> **"Victuals"**

type of bondage that; unlike slavery in Africa, in the Americus it was hereditary, inhumane, sadistic, chattel based, and perpetual in status.

Over time in our ancestral homeland, the CI destroyed and replaced much of our native languages and culture by reshaping the societal structures: social, political, and religion. Not only did they pillaged precious metals, gems, and animals, they precipitately removed other vital natural resources especially humans during what is known as the African Holocaust; "when millions died making the journey of captivity from the interior of Africa to the shores of Native Lands during the Middle Passage (Africanholicost.net)." Our Motherland would go on to be a diddled and duped supplier of the most horrific and wicked curse against humanity primordially. "Over twelve million Africans (PBS.org and Henry Louis Gates, Jr.)" would be sold or later indiscriminately stolen.  After the supply of enslaved persons had been deplete, theft of the best and most skilled, trained, and economically stable citizens began; resulting in a crippling brain drain in West Africa.  Over time, even some Kings refused to continue sales to the **avaricious invaders and conquerors of Indigenous lands**, such as the land that would become the United States of America further igniting wholesale kidnapping of any citizen deemed physically strong. Husbands stolen from the fields never to be seen again by their wives, children, and parents.

Then, unrelentingly for 13 generations or over 240 years in the Americus, a dehumanizing, sadistic, and wicked application of human bondage, subjugation and sexual violence was practiced without conscious.  Premised on oppression, mental cruelty, and extreme targeted psychological conditioning; it indoctrinated, undermined, and was mission driven to destroy the very humanity of the African.  Destroying the very humanity of the captive necessitated extreme brutal  mental and psychological conditioning. Enforced powerlessness was used to maintain control, dehumanize, psychologically cripple, and thereby

> **Chattel, Bondage, Sexual Rape and Violence, Mental Cruelty, Mental Conditioning, Oppression, Wickedness, Terrorism, Lynching**

ensure a free, totally submissive, sustainable, plentiful, cheap,  labor force.  Of equal importance was the African's genetically superior immunity to European Diseases and superior mental and physical prowess when it came to farming and invention.  The labor force was deliberately, wickedly, and sadistically programmed to service the CI"S ever-increasing dependency on human economic exploitation; as the underpinning to the emergent economic engine powered by lucrative crops of tobacco, rice, and later cotton.  It is this extreme and brutal psychological conditioning underscored by subjugation and inhumane physical brutality encapsulated with brutal and sadistic sexual violence against girls, boys, women, and men, and **its resulting mental <u>embedded remnants</u> that remain with the A-A community today that will drive the intra-community dialogue set forth in this book.**

The Nia (purpose) of this book is to ignite the mental healing of the African American people from our residual wounds by Opening Our Eyes such that we will RECOGNIZE and ADMIT our problems, Acknowledge our participation in their depth and longevity; then proceed to Heal ourselves; and henceforth, Act and React from understanding "Our Truth"; for only Truth will destroy the vestiges of Mental and Extreme Psychological Abuse that has engulfed us, and give rise to individual self-transformations leading to the unification and self-sustainability of the invincible A-A people made possible because of the grit inherited from our Ancestors. Effective self-transformations require our eyes to be "opened" to our truth and the resultant healing will initiate positive changes where needed in our family environments, in our communities, our academic focus and pursuits, to building sustainable economic infrastructures, and to engender us to advance positivity in our thoughts, words, and deeds.

Historically, despite the incessant hurling of every imaginable roadblock unleashed in the annuals of human existence against a people, <u>many</u> African-Americans have accomplished much, contributed much, and raised families that sustain themselves and live with dignity and self-respect.  Although our innate survival instincts have served us well, it is highly noticeable that throughout the African-American community, <u>some</u> in the last few generations have begun to show an underlying strain in the invincibility and focus that sustained our Ancestors such as valuing learning/education, community economic empowerment, two parent centered homes, self-respect, hard work with dignity, raising respectable and respectful children, and living every day with honor and integrity.

Yes, overall, we seem to be losing ground at an alarming rate in our communities especially in the plight of many youths, many engaging in Wanton Self-destruction sometimes even forgetting self-respect and respect for others, often failing to take advantage of educational and job opportunities that were the prayer of the Ancestors.  Many falling easy prey to drugs, guns, intra-community violence, promiscuity, and absent fathers; thereby aiding the success of the underlying well-organized campaign to permanently marginalize the A-A people.

*Today, much evil and wickedness continue to be strategically and systematically orchestrated against us,* **but the most egregious evils are things we do to ourselves and each other***.*

This internal turmoil is not lost on those who continue to treat us with distain and seek to destroy or at least marginalize us.  For example,  there was a major altercation between racial isolationists and those standing for racial justice and fairness.  I watched and listened on various media outlets as different reporters interviewed prominent members of the racial isolationist group.  Some participants voiced support for ongoing organized suppression of groups of color. When asked about A-As specifically, some replied: we do not have to worry about them because they kill each other for us all over the country.

I remembered such an outcome predicted in the **Lynch Letter** which suggested a guaranteed **recipe to remove the shackles from our ankles and place them in our heads in perpetuity,** and he projected that over time, we would begin feeding on ourselves in a **cycle of perpetual mental slavery.**  I fell to my knees and wept, then stood defiantly and said, "no more."  I must show the way out of this darkness.

In this book, I will make the case that over the ensuing years since 1865, a great many of our eyes have been closed or at best partially opened to the truth about the lingering psychological impact still embedded from the wicked time and the reality of what is required of us to build economically viable, self-sustaining, infrastructurally sound communities, and wholesome families.   If we cannot see clearly, how can we be effective in this Capitalistic Economic Structure? For so long, our eyes have been gleamed over until we are in danger of being effectively and permanently marginalized in the land of opportunity and the land of the self-anointed guardian of human rights and democratic values around the Universe. I will identify the underlying psychological condition and its impact  that has engulfed many African American (A-A) people.  It  began during the Middle Passage and has continued across the generations due to the residual effects of heredity chattel slavery. I examine this psychological condition and its resulting ongoing powerful **residual effects** today that serve as a perpetuating self-defeating disease in the African American community, which compliments the covert, overt, and subvert efforts to outright destroy us and or encourage our self-destruction.

I will expose the underlying Civil War (Population Numbers War (PNW)) that has been waged with impunity against the African American people since 1867 to ensure that our percentage of the population in this "land of the free" doesn't substantially exceed what it was at the end of the Civil War in 1865, around 13%. Then, I will remind us, the A-A people, that *"NO Validation is Necessary"* from the descendants of Colonial Imperialists, for we are Divinely whole and complete, and Validated by the blood of our Ancestors.   I will explore the historical truth that *"You Cannot Legislate the Heart"* and you certainly cannot legislate Christian hypocrisy and its underlying evils: racism, dog whistle politics, prejudice, broken class, bigotry, racial profiling, racial terrorism, generational dependency, driving while A-A, walking down a street while A-A, barbecuing while A-A, shopping while A-A, walking into your own apartment while A-A, or even playing in your community park while A-A, or simply just breathing while A-A; extreme gerrymandering, minimized weekend voting, and blatant voter supersession efforts, etc.. Underlying racial bigotry, racial terrorism  are the true reasons why the 13th, 14th, 15th, and 19th Amendments to the Constitution of the United States are often propped up with more laws: Civil Rights, Voting Rights, etc. that eventually themselves must be propped up or reauthorized as new ways to strip away our rights, undermine us at every turn, and disrespect our basic humanity and citizenship are exercised incessantly.

Next, we open our eyes and acknowledge our Truths starting with our own missteps, then remind ourselves of the egregious historical crimes against humanity from the wicked time, expose the relentless undermining efforts in play today, and examine how to reclaim our ancestral truths.  I will introduce steps to scour any generationally transmitted psychological residue, offering the path forward to healing, recovery, and redemption; leading to a new **EXPLOSION** in the mental and physical prowess of our mighty A-A people, thereby breaking out of the chains of mental slavery for all eternity.  The underlying mission here is to reclaim of our traditional greatness descended to us by our ancestors over millions of years before the B.C. Era.

I will put forth a discussion of important Political Discourse, share some Poetry for the amusement of the Griots, and finally,  I will share select A-A Historical Lore to be shared with family and friends ongoing.  Then, **With Our Eyes Opened** and seeing clearly, we can reclaim the destiny of our ancient ancestors which is to continue their early accomplishment as a great Cultural prowess before the invasion, societal and cultural destruction, theft of precious gems and natural resources, terrorism, and interruption of the Prime Directive by the CIs.

Throughout History, Colonial Imperialists and others have trampled the globe pilfering, enslaving, tricking, stealing, murdering, committing sadistic sexual terrorism, and destroying cultures; most often with a Bible in hand and Holy Prophesies being hypocritically uttered from their mouths.  Often deciding to divvy up the Natives land, even making new Countries. How different the world may be if these cultures had been allowed to develop in their own way, in their own time and were not polluted with the four poisons of greed, power, racism, and hypocrisy; and further damaged with the injection of internal turmoil pitting groups against each other.

Places like Africa, India, Egypt, Palestine, and the Americus.

## What is in a Name?

Throughout this book, I refer to us as African- Americans (A-A). I linked A-A together with a dash to show that we are African Primordially and American because of Enslavement/240 years of human bondage in the land that became the United States of America. The designation A-A recognizes and appreciates that we descend from a Developed Culture that deserves our honor and appreciation. And since we steadfastly maintain that we do not wish to be judged by the color of our skin, then we must stop teaching skin color to our children every day.  So, if we do not want to be judged by our skin's color, then it seems sensible that we stop referring to ourselves as a color.  I do not know about you, but I am not a can of paint or a Crayon.  It is high time to open our eyes and delightfully embrace our invincible culture.

We are **African-Americans (A-A)** and when we see each other reflect proudly on the fact that we are a remarkable group of survivors with grit, fortitude and invincibility having withstood every wicked, corrupt, mean-spirited and inhumane acts of terrorism and crimes against humanity ever imposed on a people in the existence of this Universe.  If the form does not have A-A, write it until we  are officially accepted as the descendants of America's Wicked Time and most egregious sin.  Use A-A to lay claim to your ancestors earned reparation.

We are the descendants who are entitled to Reparations  (compensation for historical crimes against humanity) that occurred relentlessly for over 140 years including involuntary servitude ,bondage. stolen labor, sexual terrorism, mental abuse and oppression, rape and assault, stolen language, and other unspeakable atrocities that were crimes against humanity the likes of which the world had never seen; should they ever be issued.   If it takes another 50 or 100 years, to whom will reparations be issued? There will be no way to identify the group entitled to compensation.  Using A-A indicates you can prove your lineage back to the Wicked Time between 1619 and 1865.  **We are African primordially and A-A by force.**

Adopting a permanent identification that honors our ancestors and their homeland will permanently identify the group of aggrieved who are entitle to reparations should they be considered.  The designation A-A will forever identify the descendants of one of the longest and most sadistic and wicked acts against humans in the history of the world.  The designation "Black" does not accomplish this because "Black" denotes skin color from any country.  **So, use A-A to honor our ancestors and to lay claim and identity for your descendants when America finally steps up to its responsibility and financially atone for its CRIMES Against Humanity.**

If a form does not have A-A, write it in.

## We are Africans primordial and American by force.  A-A.

<u>A-A Official Greeting</u>:  **Look the A-A brother or sistah in the eye, then flash an open favored hand once confirming that you embrace the 5Ss:  Self-worth, Self-respect, Self-determination, Self-sustainability, and Service.  Then from the depths of your life say "Harambee" (let us all pull together).  The brother or sistah will respond in kind.**

**Define things for Ourselves: U.S. Historical Period 1640-1865**

This period in United States A-A History will henceforth be referred to as **"The Wicked Time."**

## The Wicked Time:  1640-1865 CICRA.

The time when our A-A ancestors were bought or stolen from the Motherland, Africa: dehumanized, brutalized, mentally traumatized, economically exploited, reduced to chattel, and branded.  Men, women, teenage girls, and boys raped indiscriminately. Our Ancestors endured a calculated, relentless, wicked, and unwavering mission to permanently destroy our humanity, psychological health, make us mentally subservient or self-destructive forever.

*The terms Slavery does not adequately define this 240-year period in  A-A history.* *"The Wicked Time"* *more adequately describes what occurred.  Henceforth* *"The Wicked Time"* *will be used in place of slavery to describe this critical period in A-A history.*    Lcookhamilton 2019

After the Civil War,  Lincoln's death was followed by the unfavorable policies of Andrew Johnson complacent with the South's version of Reconstruction which excluded extending basic humanity to the newly freed humans.   The Federal Government of these United States of America turned a blind eye and often assisted in reintroducing some of the same policies and practices many Northerners had given their lives to change.

For example,  by denying General Sherman's Field Orders No 15 issued in January 1865 which decried that newly Freedmen be given up to Forty Acres to farm and have a homestead to be able to participate in society as equal citizens and start an Economic Infrastructure to sustain themselves.    Instead the Country stood by while de jure slavery was imposed in the form of reconstructing the South using sharecropping, lend-lease, convict-leasing, targeted hangings to instill fear, peonage; denial of job opportunities except maintaining the CI's homes and raising their children, while the slaves own children were tended to by elderly relatives or raised themselves; denial of proper health care,  and denied of voting rights.    Psychological undermining came in the form of being forced to live under imposed institutional segregation designed to underscore and mentally reinforce subjugation and degraded self-worth.

**But still we rise**.

# Chapter 1

## The Lingering Effects

## of the Stockholm Syndrome on A-As

You are not free until your mind is free. *Bob Marley told us many years ago, "emancipate yourself from Mental Slavery, none but ourselves can free our minds."*  **I maintain that many A-A people are suffering from the residual effects of the Stockholm Syndrome in its most damaging and crippling form "Mental Slavery."**  WWW. *African holoaust.net* defines Mental Slavery as a state of mind where discerning between *liberation* and *enslavement* is twisted.  Where one becomes trapped by misinformation about self and the world.  Mental Slavery is far more sinister than physical slavery because the chains are invisible and are transmitted across generations. Let us define the syndrome, identify the evidence of its psychologically mind-altering effects, examine the triggering experience(s), then give confirmation of the existence of the syndrome in too many A-A's psychics today.

> **Remember, we the A-A people did not land on Plymouth Rock. Plymouth landed on us.**  Malcolm X
>
> **The Clotilda and Africatown**

Several sources define the <u>Stockholm Syndrome:</u>

Britannica.com -Stockholm syndrome, a psychological response wherein a captive begins to <u>identify closely</u> with his or her captors, as well as with their <u>agenda and</u> demands.

Merriam-Webster:  The psychological tendency of a hostage to bond with, identify, or sympathize with his or her captor.  <u>Www.meriam</u> webster.com.

*For example,*  house slaves sometimes responded when the Master was ill "Masser, how sick are **we** today?"

**How did the Stockholm Syndrome Develop in the A-A Psychic between 1640  -1865?**

[www.bbc.com/news/magazine-22447726](www.bbc.com/news/magazine-22447726) Kathryn Wescott.    Explains the …irrational feelings of some captives for their captors per Frank Ochberg.  Here is what happens:

1. *People experience something terrifying that just comes at them out of the blue.  They are certain they are going to die. The mental effects of experiencing something terrifying that comes suddenly can be lasting and devastating.*

   *A-As* being stolen in slave raids for example or sold away from their homeland by their own leaders; away from family, language, traditions; and packed in the bowel of a ship without adequate sanitation for over a month.  Forced to watch as many were fed to sharks, brought to a strange land, forbidden to communicate, shackled and chained, sold to strangers, forced to work from sun to sun, raped without discrimination, branded, required to wear a yoke, dehumanized and beaten without mercy to ensure control and for daring to speak in native tongue, or for not being totally submissive.  We suffered such severe mental, physical, and sexual abuse for thirteen generations.  Enslaved men were made to KOWTOW and grovel day after day as women and children looked on, in effect, emasculating the man.  This indeed qualifies as experiencing a sudden severely terrifying mental, physical, and emotional experience that would traumatize and damage the psychic of most humans.

2. *They (in this instance, slaves) experience a type of infantilization where like a child, they are unable to eat, speak or go to the toilet without permission.*

This infantilization and dehumanization began on the ships around 1640, as captives were only allowed to eat and officially relieve oneself with permission or by soiling oneself and the person next to you leaving you to lay in human waste including female issues… Yoked and ankles chained, knowing that if you became ill, you would be fed to sharks was mentally grueling.  Sailors reported you could see blood for miles behind a slave ship as sharks were in active pursuit of live bodies being tossed overboard. While over 12 million African citizens were shipped to the Americas, only roughly 10 million survived the journey.

Again, infantilization continued over 246 years through 13 generations in these United States of America.  As part of the infantilization, the A-A male was referred to as "boy" even in advanced age.

Imagine A-A human beings were born, lived their entire lives, and died in submission to a CHATTEL SYSTEM and most often a physical and sexual abuser who hypocritically dawned the church pews every Sunday.  Open Your Eyes and see that ironically today, many still lead services and so-called believers dawn the pews every Sunday yet practice racism, bigotry, and ungodliness in their hearts and in their actions.   While projecting to live based on the teaching  that demands love thy neighbor as thyself and what ye sow so shall ye reap.

After the Civil War, infantilization continued to be widely imposed. A-As were not supposed to look a European American directly in the eye less he/she get slapped or worse.  The so-called Freedmen were subjected to extreme segregation, black codes, denied self-supporting economic opportunities, vagrancy laws, extreme bigotry, lynching violence, and overall racial terrorism.  This forced the status of former slaves to be free but not free.

3. *Over time "… they(slaves) are in denial that the <u>captor</u> (Colonial Imperialist) is the person who put them in that situation.  In the <u>captive's</u> (slave's) mind, <u>they think the captor is the person who is going to let them live. </u>"*

In the case of A-As, there were over 246 years of mental programming where, to stay alive, you swallowed your dignity, suppressed your manhood, allowed yourself to be raped at will, both women and men; your children to be sold away, provided merciless free labor from dawn to dust six days a week, forced to eat a diet of the unhealthiest foods, wear harsh inferior clothing, and experience the scourge indiscriminately. Your religion, language and traditions were beaten out of you and finally to reinforce dignity denied and underscore complete mental submission and powerlessness, the slave was not allowed to raise his head when responding to or addressing someone of the European culture.  The **captive (slave)** buried the dehumanization, powerlessness, shame, and hurt deep inside resulting in self-hatred and an unnatural affinity to please the abuser...

The **captive** wants to live and psychologically accepts the more he/she pleases the **captor or Colonial Imperialist (CI)** by adopting his ways, submitting to his sexual exploits, loving what he loves, hating what he hates including self; and tattling on others will ensure the likelihood of his/her survival.  <u>This tattling and backbiting introduced the mistrust and crab-mentality that permeates the A-A culture today.</u>

Over time, shackles and chains were no longer needed.  The mental conditioning, dehumanization and oppression was such that, for the most part, captives no longer ran away.  Like an undisturbed parasitic tape worm with its self-producing segments slowly taking over, we began to feed on each other with envy, mistrust and self-hate which continues to undermine our communities to this very day.

Then, there are the mental effects of prolonged sexual exploitation, forced sexual accommodation, and sexual violence most harshly forced on teenage girls, then women, men, and boys; yes, men and boys. Because of the fear of death or brutal inhumane lashings, starvation, or hanging; the slave women would begin teaching coping mechanisms to their daughters and girls approaching the teenage years. Men and fathers physically and mentally compromised by brutality and sadistic abuse, were forced to turn away as their daughter, wife, and or son, was taken away to be used as a sex toy for the slave owner or overseer, etc.  Over time, the girl, woman, and boy will begin to view the adult male slave as weak, engendering a lack of respect between the male figure, women, and children.  Over generations, this seething disrespect does serious underlying damage to the psychic of the A-A woman's  respects for the man. Even to this day, all too often, the A-A woman will subliminally become the man of the house and proceed to act that way which confuses the children, undermines the natural role of the male, and often makes the boy child weak.

4.     Over time, the **captive** begins to identify with and view the **captor** as righteous and their savior and begin to emulate the captive's view of beauty, religion, truth, even begin to hate what the captor hates including hating self, those that look like self, including self-

physical attributes. Thus, the mental effects of the transposition of self-image to value the image and attitude of the capturer.

The physiological underpinning was to remake the soul of the slave by removing attachments such as language, culture, beliefs, religion, and tribal/family structure to traumatize the soul. As time passed, the slave/captive taught his/her own children to *value* the captor/master's ways over himself.  The abuser's physical looks became our idea of beauty and is still shamefully emulated my many A-As today.   Right from the womb, many captives began to teach their children self-hatred about their hair, skin tone, by using verbal put-downs, and racial name calling, and embracing degrading stereotypes used to indoctrinate and disparage.

Further, our native tongue ceased to even be spoken in private.  We adopted the captor's version of religious practice as our own and with even more fidelity.   There were severe deep mental and emotional effects on the family structure as children were often sold away from their mothers perhaps leading to generational detachment disorders.

5.    *Impact of Longevity in captivity.*

 In many documented cases of the Stockholm Syndrome, the captive was released after a relatively short duration: several days, two weeks, and for some nearly 10 years.  Yet, severe mental and emotional scars were inflicted in weeks or days.  In comparison, our A-A Ancestors endured 13 generations, held captive for over 240 years, while being brutalized, raped, dehumanized, and forced to watch others being brutalized and even hung. The enslaved children observed and witnessed the adults pleasing the enslaver in every dehumanizing, demoralizing, and self-hating way.  They watched the accommodators, backbiters, and tattlers, who even today, undermine their own people. As they are still rewarded with being labeled a good ________.  The message has always been clear: to be a good person in the site of my abuser, I must undermine my own people, commit severe abuse to my hair  and skin to show my self-hatred,  run and tattle, then quite often neglect to teach my children their history and overwhelming ancestorial contributions to the economic success of this country, say degrading and demeaning things to my children  "good hair, bad hair," while trying to get the terrorist abuser's approval.

To underscore, consider we were enslaved by the Colonial Imperialists for around 246 years in what became the United States.  Our language, labor stolen, and dignity denied, our men's manhood taken before the eyes of their children. Teenage girls and boys, men and women raped with impunity or forced into sexual accommodation on command; babies sold from their mothers, skin branded like the livestock, considered inhuman but chattel; extended the worst kinds of human brutality to be inflicted, Institutionalized emotional and physical abuse, being forced to watch severe physical abuse or murder against those attempting to escape or refusing to accommodate with work or sex, men not being able to protect their wives and daughters;  severe isolation regulated to the plantation only, forced to live for generations in fear and in terror, subjected to mental cruelty designed to engender self-hatred, and induce religious practice indoctrination.

**Incidents in the Life of a Slave Girl by**

Harriet Anne Jacobs

Open your eyes. The truth is our ancestors being held as defacto prisoners of war and in captivity for hundreds of years resulted in the most egregious form of the mental and physical cruelty, sexual terrorism, and economic exploitation was deliberately applied to destroy our mental prowess and willpower.  It continued in other forms after the Wicked Time: institutionalized segregation, blatant racism, injustice, and other covert  and overt strategies engaged to deny and undermine our humanity, economic advancement, and right to equal justice.

The prolonged imbedded effect of the Stockholm Syndrome naturally reverberated down through the generations after the Emancipation Proclamation and the ensuring Reconstruction of the South which was premised on maintaining the A-A as close to slavery as possible by providing very limited employment opportunities other than cleaning, cooking, gardening, raising the former CI's children, and later sharecropping.

6.      *Reinforced Demeaning Imaging, and Family Break-ups*

Psychologically, sadistic beatings, maiming's, hangings, children sold away, brutal rapes and cruel  subservient messaging such as not be able to hold your head up while addressing the CI, when experienced daily, can without realization, begin to operate just below the consciousness mind and lodge in the subconscious mind.  That is why it was so necessary for the CI to troll every aspect of our Ancestors' existence and undermine their dignity and self-worth daily at the most fundamental levels.  The institutionalized goal was complete indoctrination to the point where one would believe negative images of self, and overtime, even begin to teach such demeaning imaging to their children and we have done just that for a long time.

7. ***Ritualistic Murders as a Spectator Sport.***

Often official notice went out in advance ensuring the murder of an A-A became a spectator sport to be witnessed by the community, even children. It served to instill horror, fear, psychological conditioning, and total submission in the slave/captive, and unbridled superiority in the minds of the CI and his/her children.  The children of the CI could watch the spectator sport unfold which taught them the life of a slave did not  have value, was not to be respected, and it could be ruthlessly exploited at will.

Even many years after the Civil War ended, such Community Rituals continued.  One such horrific murderous episode was the murder of Willie Brown, who in 1919, Omaha, Nebraska was burned alive as the European American (EA) community gleefully watched with their children.  Again, lynching as a Spectator Sport was a source of entertainment for hundreds of years.   Imagine that …

8. ***A Mental Undermining Dichotomy.***

The contradiction had to weigh on the Captives mind, being entrusted with the Captor's most precious possessions their children and taking care of their household including preparing their meals.  We raised their children with our warmth, love, and trained them to adulthood.  We were responsible for cooking, serving, and preserving the food they ate.  We even breast fed their children at times, not to mention cared for family members during sickness.  Think about this for a minute:  imagine we prepared the Captor's food, performed their domestic maintenance, nursed, and treated them with medicine we often concocted as herbal remedies based on knowledge and training from the

Motherland.  Imagine nursing them to wellness, while at the same time, unconscionable wickedness was being done to us and perpetuated against us in perpetuity including enduring their sadistic sexual abuse.   How much sexual abuse?  Just look around at our many skin colors.   I can hear the slave quietly ask, "Why do you hate me so, and yet your baby drinks from my breast?" "You eat the food my hands prepare, and you trust me even to give you medicine." How conflicted must they have felt while hand washing the soiled monthly rags for the females to reuse during the following monthly cycle.  The cruelty and agony inflicted from the situation had to be beyond most human capacity.  But we survived.

9.      *Exposure to European Diseases.*

We came into contact for the first time with European diseases such as smallpox, measles, and influenza, etc.  We became exposed to these diseases while interacting with the CI.  These are the same diseases that nearly wiped out the Native American population thus precipitating the focus on using African slave labor because our mental and physical prowess far outperformed indentured servitude and native enslavement.  It was the natural invincibility of the Africans mental and physical prowess that attracted the CI to the adaptability of the African as the best fit to supply stolen labor to the emerging economy that become the United States.

**Ida B. Wells**
Crusader Against Lynching

**Philando Castile**

After the Emancipation Proclamation, we continued to work in their homes and raise their children because there were no jobs for the newly freed.  Not providing economic opportunities for the newly freed aided the determination of Southerners to keep A-As as close to human bondage as possible which was allowed and emboldened by the attitude of the Andrew Johnson and several subsequent Administrations.  Imagine we continued to prepare their  food,  nurse their children, nurse them when they were sick, and perform their domestic maintenance while at the same time, unconscionable wickedness was being perpetuated against our people in the form of convict leasing, loitering ordinances, black codes, peonage, segregation, racial terrorism, inferior schools; restricted land ownership, poor housing availability leading to sharecropping, which was slavery by another name; and fear mongering horrors employed by the KKK that could only be derived from the wickedness of the soul.  These things were coupled with covert and overt rejections of full citizenship and segregation and with intended injustices in perpetuity. Such became part of the residual psychologically damaging and mentally undermining way of life for the A-As, who were already suffering from the loss of self-worth indoctrinated during the development of the Stockholm syndrome.

# Chapter 2

# Evidence of Lingering Manifestations
# of the Stockholm Syndrome

How do the residual effects of the Stockholm Syndrome continue to manifest itself in the

psychic of many A-As during the 154 years since the end of the Civil War?  It is these residual

mental effects that causes us to undermine ourselves,  many kill each other without conscious,

many destroy our communities, and willingly help with our marginalization.  Here are a few:

*1.*    **The Words We Use and Our Attitude Towards Each Other.**

All too often we hurl the same racial slurs at each other as the CI employed to taunt,

humiliate, and belittle our ancestors.  Disrespecting of self and self-loathing are a clear

example of the Stockholm Syndrome residually manifesting itself across generations

especially in how we embrace self-hatred so engrained that our minds are mentally

crippled enough to refer to each other using the most horrific and insulting names even

those used to belittle and humiliate our ancestors.  Ask yourself, why would I adopt the

same insults toward by brothers that were used to humiliate by forefathers?  Stupid and

a depiction of slavery in the mind.  Further, look at the blatant disrespect, downright

hostility, and violence we exhibit towards each other all too often.

## 2.    The Crab-Mentality.

Exercised throughout our communities today leading to, among other things, our failure to support community-based business infrastructure and capital investment.  The "pull you down instead of build you up" actions have almost wiped out grass roots economics in our communities.  Have you noticed; we are the only culture who often do not support their own people by frequenting their businesses first?   We smilingly spend our money with other cultures who are entrepreneur minded enough to set-up shop in our neighborhoods, but the money does not remain there to circulate and contribute value.  This is catastrophic economically to any community.

Our brothers and sistahs from the West Indies, Central America, Mexico, and Puerto Rico do a far better job of infrastructure development while actively and deliberately supporting their own businesses and each other (Ujamma).

## 3.    Seeking Validation

Our misguided overarching needs to be validated by the CI during the Wicked Time, has remained to present day as many A-As continue to seek approval from European Americans (EA) or measure their self-worth by European standards.  This misguided need to please the abuser started during the Wicked Time and has led to misguided directions and wasted opportunities.  We have measured our worth and success by whether we can live next to, play with, attend school with, and socialize with the European Americans (EA).  We have seemingly failed to recognize that because an idea, suggestion, or a neighborhood is embraced by Europeans Americans does not automatically make it enviable or worthy, or that we should go chasing after it at the expense of developing and building our own. For many, the values of our daily existence are seen through EA lenses.   See Chapter 3.

A few years ago, in a small town in the deep South, South Koreans moved in to open a plant.   The Country Club was and still is segregated.   The Koreans did not go to court or take to the streets,  trying to force acceptance, they built their own Country Club and Golf Course.  This is the correct attitude.  Through cooperative economics, they earned respect, and displayed courage and self-sustainability before their children and the world.

**4.      Engaging in Wanton Self-destruction.**

Too many of us wantonly destroy ourselves generation after generation by epidemically engaging in A-A on A-A crime, much of it A-A young men killing each other;  high health-risk behaviors including excessive eating (gluttony), consumption of low energy processed foods, substance abuse, excessive alcohol and tobacco consumption, multi-generational welfare, many failing to  parent erudite and self-respecting children, and other self-defeating tendencies that ultimately take over and control our lives.  Too many have become mentally and physically lethargic, and most severely damaging, is our failure to build and support sustainable economic infrastructure in our communities.

**5.      Multi-generational Living on the Dole.**

Living on the Dole is to be use as a short-term bridge in times of distress.  For example, in case of job loss, sudden death, temporary economic hardship, etc. It is nothing to be ashamed of and many families have reached out and used Public Assistance in its varied forms as a bridge until they could pull themselves up by their bootstraps. Open your eyes, the Welfare bridge for A-As  is strategically not designed for the family to recover, gain living wage employment, find affordable housing, have access to quality daycare and schools. It is designed to trap a family in a cycle of poverty, crime, negative home environments, food apartheid, crime infested neighborhoods and inferior public educational opportunities.          It is a tool in the well-orchestrated plan to marginalize the A-A people.

While welfare is a viable short-term solution in a crisis, we all know *some adults* are teaching generations that to work to support yourself and your family is not wholesome and desirable perpetuating a cycle of dependency. When multiple generations in the same linage have lived their entire existences reaching for a hand-out that is not designed to be a hands-up, it leads to false expectations, mostly unproductive adults, a climate of distress in neighborhoods, and substandard schools.  Besides, there is no such thing as a free lunch. Somebody somewhere must pay and not just the working taxpayer.  Over generations, you pay by losing your dignity and self-worth, while at the same time, crippling your children by not modeling self-sufficiency, self- sustainability, and hard work. There are major consequences to a so-called free ride on the system including the underlying deliberate destruction of the A-A Family.   Understand the Welfare System as

<table>
<tr><td colspan="3">Generational <u>Welfare</u></td></tr>
<tr><td>W</td><td>=</td><td>Whittling away at your dignity and self-respect</td></tr>
<tr><td>E</td><td>=</td><td>Ethos Depletion</td></tr>
<tr><td>L</td><td>=</td><td>Low Self-esteem</td></tr>
<tr><td>F</td><td>=</td><td>False Expectations</td></tr>
<tr><td>A</td><td>=</td><td>Apathy, Anger, Aggression</td></tr>
<tr><td>R</td><td>=</td><td>Reliance on Others Instead of Self over generations</td></tr>
<tr><td>E</td><td>=</td><td>Emotional Abuse</td></tr>
</table>

meaded out to our people is a systematic and willful intent to destroy  the A-A family as a self-sustaining unit.

For example, reason would suggest that since a welfare mother does not have to work, she will raise some of the most well-behaved and educationally focused children in public schools, volunteer and participate in PTA, PTO.  This is often not the case.  As a matter of fact, in too many cases, the opposite is true.  This is a good indication of how destructive the cycle of dependency imparts on our community especially the youth who often miss out on a fair chance at no fought of their own.  We must choose to change this behavior now.  It is up to us to become self-reliant people for the sake of future generations.  Here is another enigma.  Why is it that in many instances, children of welfare and food stamp receiving mothers, show up at school unfed and missing school supplies?  Some schools even send a snack home to ensure the child has food over the weekend.   Many of these children often behave badly, and act out in anger, speak poorly, and diminish the classroom rigor for all students in the class.  This is unfair to the students willing and wanting to learn at the highest level possible.

> **Find out just what any people will quietly submit to and you have the exact measure of the injustice and wrong which will be imposed on them, and these will continue until they are resisted with words or blows or both.**
>
> **The limits of tyrants are prescribed by the endurance of those whom they oppress.**
>
> **Frederick Douglas**

While any of us could need assistance due to sudden economic hardship, consider whether generational dependency  is the example you want for your children and grandchildren, for it usually becomes a form of mental slavery.

But know that when it comes to Welfare in this Country, the amounts spent on the "poor", in no way compares to the excessive amounts in trillions handed out in tax breaks and bailouts to business, the top 5% of the population, to the Agricultural Sector, and others who have been receiving subsidies in the billions forever.  Corporate Welfare is designed to help recipients either recover and or become wealthier, but most often simply given as political favors.  No stigma attached to **"Corporate Welfare."**   No considering that "you" are a Welfare recipient same as someone in the Projects.  But it is the same.  Taxpayer dollars given freely.  The difference is **Intention. Welfare issued in distressed communities is intended to trap the people and their future generations in a  cycle of  poverty, rundown neighborhoods, substandard educational opportunities, and overall mental slavery.**  While those receiving Corporate Welfare in the form of tax breaks, tax loopholes,  and bail outs; subsidies to farmers, etc.  just ride the gravy train of tax payer dollars with glee and feel embolden by the unfair and unjust application of policies across the nation entrapping the middle class and further distressing already distressed communities.

Corporate tax breaks, corporate handouts, the writing of  laws that give favor and tax breaks for the top 5% including bail-outs, continue to be meaded out while the Congress ignores infrastructure development and repairs,  a disgracefully deficient public education system in certain zip codes, fails to extend free public post-secondary education, fails to allow the average citizen access to safe and quality childcare, and provide access to health care at least comparable to what those elected to office receive.

It is time people realize that **A-As are not the largest Welfare recipients** by group in this country by far.  Just do the numbers and see for yourself.  But to malign us,  this yolk is always put around our necks.  But let us agree to do a better job at self-sufficiency for the sake of our children and the generations to come.

> *If we hate ourselves then, who will love us?*

6.     **Some A-A Men Acting as Sperm Donors and not Fathers.**

While some A-A men work hard and strive to be the best providers and fathers to their children, too many make babies they do not parent or financially support, often relegating them to unsafe and unhealthy homes, and most cruel, often leaving these children to the mercy of the governmental system whose goal is the destruction of the A-A family unit and by default, the children. This abomination is an insult to nature and a slap in the face of the Ancestors and creates a severely negative cloud of energy in our communities.

Some A-A men are very responsible fathers, husbands, and citizens, because they had such an example growing up.  But a large portion do not know how to be productive and responsible men and fathers because of poor to no examples in their early lives, and the cycle continues.  In many households, the woman is the central figure and often saddled with the role of both mom and dad.  A woman cannot teach a boy how to be a man.  As stated earlier, boys need a man, a real man (father, provider, and respecter of women) as the example of how to support, love, respect, and care for a family, and not a leech of an example that lays up with the mother and contributes little to the household that is constructive.

**7.** **Imitation is the Greatest Form of Flattery.**

Ask yourself is it true?  Do we try to look like, dress like, and live alongside EA, less we feel we have not succeeded?  For over 150 years since the Civil War, A-As, have degraded and compromised our dignity to impose European values and ideas on ourselves.  We bleached our skin to become as close to the captor's as possible.  Even today, many in the A-A community still see a "light skinned" person as more beautiful. Some A-A men will not date a dark-skinned A-A woman and will proudly tell you so, and vice versa.

And over the same 150 years, we have fried, applied lye-based products, permed, glued, sewed, and continue to spend countless billions on anything sold in the marketplace  to make our hair resemble the CI's.  This teaches inferiority to our own children instead of self-love and ancestral appreciation.  For example, "she has good hair," with inference to another child that her hair is bad or referred to as nappy because she looks her **authentic self** and does not adopt the look of the CI.  This "good hair obsession" instills self-loathing, instead of self-worth in our children; and it will grow up in them making them angry teenagers because we program them from birth to value someone else's features, hair, skin, and general looks.  This contributes to the unmooring of our children.   Nappy is a good thing; it means the hair is extraordinarily strong.

Recently, I had such an experience with my granddaughter.  Around the age of two, we began to buy her ethnic dolls along with popular EA offerings.  Without realizing it,  even though the ethnic dolls for the most part were of the same skin hue as she is, the hair texture was not.  The hair texture and style said to her that her hair should be straight and long. If our little girls sit around combing long straight hair in their doll collections, they may value and deem beautiful hair as long and straight, leaving no room to appreciate their own beautiful coffers.  My granddaughter said, "Granny I want my hair to look like hers" and pointed to the long European textured hair on the doll.   I froze. Let this be a lesson to us all.  Our girls need to play with dolls and hair that represent their reality.  Our youth need an anchor as to who they are as a person, and that they were born worthy as they Divinely entered this universe.  We immediately corrected and went out of our way to find mor dolls with afros or natural hair, etc.

> **Mental Slavery will be headed for defeat when A-A women cease going so far as to use the nuclear option in attempt to straighten their hair.**

We must never forget our hair is a symbol and source of our strength and glory.  Those of you who choose to wear locks or authentic hair, keep it neat in honor of our ancestors. Lately, there has been a recurrence of something that transpired in the 1960's and early 70's.  Some A-A females have come to realize we are free to appreciate and wear our own Divinely given hair. That it is beautiful and wearing it sets you free.  Yes, our authentic selves set us free.  *Feel the freedom ladies!  Teach this freedom to our young girls by example.*

## 8.     Brown Paper Bag Test.

For generations in our own communities before 1955, many dark-skinned A-A were not encouraged to attend Colleges and Universities or apply for certain professional jobs if they could not pass the paper bag test.  If your skin was darker than a paper bag, you need not apply.   The closer you resembled the slave master, often the better the opportunities abound in society and sadly often among our own people.  By not embracing, respecting, and loving our own physical attributes, we deliver an underlying message to our children that physical attributes of the European Americans are to be valued over our own.  This communicates self-hatred to children and steers them to grow up hating themselves and to continue the cycle of self-hatred with their own children.  Combine this with the perpetual attempts to impede our civil and human rights, disfranchise us, and downright overt disrespect shown for the lives of African American men and boys even in their own back yards; helps undermine the self-worth of A-A adolescents as they grow into teenagers in such a racially profiling society.   In other words, these children do not get the platform on which to be properly anchored in adulthood.  They will in turn pass on the same self-doubts and confusion about who they are to their children and the cycle continues.

## 9.     We are Quick to Embrace Wickedness.

In the A-A community, whatever **wickedness** arises in society, we tend to grab on to it in mass and take it to an extreme which is often its most destructive impact.

Much of the self-hatred, degradation, and violence being fed to our children is in disguise and often at the hands of our own people.  If you research the true <u>majority ownership</u> of some supposed to be ethnic entities that spew cultural norms into our communities (radio stations, recording labels,  networks, some online formats, , etc.); you might be surprised at the identify of some of the true puppeteers.  Sometimes we participate in orchestrating unacceptable and self-insulting behaviors, undignified dress; blatantly hostile and self-hating rhetoric, wickedly violent, rude, loud and undignified interactions; while often glorifying A-A on A-A violence, promiscuity with over sexualized social norms, and overall poor character  traits.  And this is what our children watch and listen  to as our norms .  We are the only culture that deliberately feed such negativities to our own children.   After what we have been through, is this the type of messaging we need to send our young girls and boys? **They are watching**.  We should be ashamed of ourselves.  Allowing our young to be led to slaughter with such behaviors, hostile and belittling language, and ways of dressing we do not want for our own children and grandchildren.    My people, we have a responsibility to recognize the wolf in sheep's clothing.

> **Read the Lynch Letter**
>
> **on every January 1st**

10. **Projecting Negativity to the world in our Limited Entertainment Roles and Opportunities**.

In terms of A-A men in movies, for years most died the most horrific deaths, and many were often portrayed as criminals, snitches, unemployed, consumers of mind-altering substances, and lacking sexual impropriety.  Often, costumed as grotesquely as possible.  Notice how in most Hi-Fi movies and shows, the weird, evil,  strange person or group is usually of non-European pigmentation.  And in general, the same  can be said about unfavorable portrayals of A-A women over the years.  They were often portrayed as loud, angry, argumentative, promiscuous,  ladies of the evening, and without morals.

That is why , *Posse, The Cosby Show,  Blackish, The Black Panther,  BlackKlansman, Fat Albert, Julia, 227, The Fresh Prince, A Different World, and The Green Book, Malcolm X,  works by Ava DuVernay,  Chadwick Bozeman,  and  many others*  have  held  out  such  promise  and encouragement  to  the  A-A  community  as  they  are  premised  on  dignity,  self-worth,  good character traits, and present our community in an aspirational light to our youth, and we are grateful.

The  truth  of  the  matter,  there  are  far  more  drug  addicts  with  access  to  illegal  drugs  and acquisition  and  consumption  of  illegal  drugs  in  the  EA  communities.   But  you  do  not  see  this replicated or accurately portrayed in crime series, police dramas, leading roles in movies, or the news media.  Such portrayals are usually assigned to persons of color but mostly A-As.

## 11.    A-A Mothers Over-Mothering A-A Boys.

Another residual effect of the Stockholm Syndrome began as A-A females and mothers  learned to cope with Lynching always trying to protect the male child or her husband by shielding or pushing him behind her.  Often, leaving her bed to service the enslaver/abuser to keep her family safe.   This  is  unnatural  and  compromises  the  woman's  dignity  and  self-respect;  and  without realizing it, over time, the female will feel little to no respect for the man who cannot protect her.  Today, many are still trying to protect the son instead of allowing him to stand and grow into a productive man, making many weak.

After generations of A-A women, often subconsciously, trying to protect the A-A man or son, the result is a very destructive role reversal permeating our community. Children observe and live through these role reversals and the cycle perpetuates.

Resultingly, if we A-A women are not careful, many of us will continue to raise strong daughters and often love many sons to weakness, while making endless excuses for their inadequacies and failures to thrive. A boy needs a strong, *genuine family man* to model for him how to be a man, treat a woman, and take care of a family.

**12.    Too Many Unhealthy Home Environments.**

Think about it, in far too many homes, a lack of respect and appreciation for one's own body is taught as some A-A women parade man after man before their children. How many different men should your children see you wake up with in the mornings in your home? What values, self-respect, and dignity are you teaching your children? The daughter often grows up and does the same: find an unproductive leech to take advantage of her. And the boy grows up to have no respect for women and use them the same way his mother was used. The cycle continues and has continued for generations. Enough is enough. Respect yourself and your children will grow up to respect themselves.

Then there is the danger many of our youth experience daily by the mere fact that they are in urban areas that are panopticons to police departments. They are racially profiled at every turn, harassed, and incarcerated unnecessarily to fight crime, but necessary if the goal is to force a felony so his/her voice which is  their vote can be silence.

**13.    A-A Young Men Hating and Killing Each Other.**

Although our A-A males are awesome and endowed with great mental and physical prowess, many are killing each other daily without a conscious the same as the slave master did for over 240 years.  They have become their own version of white hooded murderers that come in the day or night.   Self-hatred programming has been so successful that we have become our own lynch mob. This is how deep mental slavery has developed in our psychic.  We are feeding on ourselves. To die is easy. Ask yourself, "Why am I afraid to live? Why are you killing your own brothers?  Are you so mentally weak and manipulated that you let wickedness get in your head and corrupt your mind to where you will, without thought or hesitation, and in an act of self-hatred, destroy your own brothers and by extension their families often including small children left behind?"

Have you stopped to consider how ironic it is that  many of our  communities and neighborhoods do not have access to fresh fruits, vegetables,  oils, and in general quality foods that are not processed with things that kill over time, but handguns are everywhere. We do not own any factories that make guns, trucks, ships, or plans that transport them. So how do you suppose they show up on the streets of our communities so readily available as a killing tool to be use by us against each other.  The trap is set, and we fall in like sheep led to slaughter.

It happens and has been happening or I should say orchestrated for over 100 years.  That is the deliberate, calculated efforts to take advantage of our mental slavery to self-hate and thereby be weak enough to be bamboozled into killing our own.

# Killing My Own

by lcookhamilton

Terrorists no longer need come during the dark of night

With white sheets and lights burning bright

Just pay me to spout hateful lyrics at my own brothers

And sneakily surround me with some colors.

Flash a little cash, some sneakers, and bling

And I will Kill what looks like me right there on the scene.


Because I am too blind to see.

You supplied the guns and ammo to me with glee

Then you laugh and discuss again with a friend

"That  I will never be free

Cause I stupidly stay under your knee"

Mad at my own instead of being mad at thee

And you gloat while I gleefully Kill my own

**But even a fool knows that killing your own  is wickedly wrong.**

Why? Just think, there are scientists around the globe experimenting with rewriting the code of life in a petri dish including genetic modification, others working on artificial intelligence, augmented reality, zig, interplanetary travel, advanced diagnostic tools in healthcare, electro plasmonic, all kinds of algorithms,  still other engineers are heavily engaged on new frontiers involving cyber security and cyber war, CRISPR gene-editing;  and climate reality, while you are foolishly running around shooting each other.  Stop being senseless and a mental slave, sending your brothers to an early grave.

To be fair, I can relate to the anger and disappointment many youths in our communities live with daily.  Since WWI, many youths have grown up watching their families live in squalid conditions enhanced with plantation style policing. Our youth cried out: "You adults embraced a path that has not resulted in the equality promised. You, with your yes sir and yes mam, begging, marching, suing in court, racially profiled at every turn; dying in war after war yet still disrespected and treated unequally. Why, we are not even safe walking down the street, even in our own back yards, walking into our own apartment, or napping in the lounge of the Ivy League School we attend."

We as parents,  tell our youth how great they are and to work hard and reach their potential.  Then almost diametrically when, even as young children, they are out with their family, they witness blatant disregard for their parents' rights during the almost daily encounters with the occupying police force in their communities.  This creates a conflict within the child growing up that he/she cannot resolve which leads to misplaced rage and anger and that his/her parents cannot protect them.

Living under occupation or panopticon for generations as a way of life, witnessing the limited success of marches and court challenges couple with the residual effects of generations of passed down self-hatred that is reverberating throughout our culture, it is no wonder that youth had enough and decided to speak in a genre that exposed the true conditions and despair they were living and seeing all around them.

Further, today's crisis of A-A on A-A gun violence is because over the generations, enslaved youth grew up under the same indoctrination to please the enslaver and hate their innate selves as exhibited by their parents.  They learned to almost transform their entire natural instincts and value system to what is pleasing and valued by EAs.  Hence, the same misplaced values have been subliminally and overtly passed down through the generations which merely continues today to emasculate and abuse them. Imagine the scaring that has occurred to their mental, emotional, psychological, well-being over generations.



The takeaway is sometimes in dismay, we have watched the anger, internal turmoil, disappointments, and the underlying residual self-hatred begin to rage as told in the outcry of the last few generations in their music. Perhaps it should not have shocked us that the pants were lowered and the lyrics sometimes shocking and raw. The youth cried out, "Adults, we are tired, we listened to your way:  again, you marched, you sung, you prayed, you sued in courts, you saluted the flag, many of you died defending the flag; and yet you failed to secure for us:

equal rights, equal justice, quality public education, free and fair elections, and humane treatment in our neighborhoods."

And so they spoke their truth, perhaps the truth about the conditions they were enduring in broken communities, many with broken families, broken schools, broken living environments, broken injustice system, and broken glass policing which equated to being under occupation and harassment for generations underscored by watching generations of decay and subjected to the well-organized efforts to supply the Prison Industrial Complex with cheap labor, and the municipal coffers with inflated revenue earned on the backs of those with the least.  But their truth has only led to more death, destruction, crippling of our communities, prison overcrowding, and loss of voting rights for many.   A new truth about redemption, self-love and self-sustainability must be spoken by our youth.  And they are up to the task.

## 14.    Self-hatred Transmitted Residually from The Wicked Time

Embedded self-hatred and its underpinning conflict with self-worth is why we shoot each other down without regard for life and why we willfully send our own brethren to an early grave. It is the same reason we sell each other toxic drugs to provide a mental escape, mistreat and degrade our girls and women, and then become slaves to the prison industrial complex.  Therefore, today we need more genuine MEN standing tall as the central figure in the family instead of sitting around day after day talking loudly and saying nothing and trying to scheme the "System."  In the end, the only thing that gets schemed is you and the generations behind you.

## 15.    *Negative Messaging.*

Across industries, media, and markets, we have an individual responsibility to teach, sing, or talk positive messaging of self-esteem, self-worth, self-sustainability, and positive pursuits.  We must never willingly put forth messaging about hating each other, degrading females, killing each other, engaging in promiscuity, and indecent exposure of our body parts; for this negative and poisonous messaging is simply slavery by another name, and in fact, doing the bidding of those out to marginalize us. Deliberate negative messaging is why the entertainment industry often project many A-A women and girls as loud, scantily clad, abrasive, promiscuous, undignified, angry, on generational welfare, and with multiple baby daddies.   Even Casting Directors seem to overly cast certain ethnic groups as the brains and the African American male is often cast as  the clown, criminal, snitch,  or some other role that often does not allow portrayal of the exceptional mental capabilities of the A-A male.

If we are a participants in deleterious messaging across any platform, we serve **as a malevolent surrogate towards our own people**, and it suggest we are mentally damaged enough to present to the world negative messaging and images to reinforce deliberately degrading stereotypes.

**You must stop engaging in, and the rest of us stop going along with, such self-hatred and destructive practices.  Know that Cause and Effect is Absolute.  If you are guilty of having participated in this self-destruction of our community.  If you are guilty of spewing self-destructive anger, and hatful violent filled mental hype and lyrics to your own brethren and humanity, you are the devil in disguise controlled and sent by the man with the white sheet hood ever so sly.  The stupidity of it is enough to make me cry,  to make cry.**

<u>Accountability</u>

**Those of you who participated in the internal destruction of our youth over the last twenty years,  help to poison their minds towards <u>self-hatred</u>, hatred of each other, and glamorized riddling many of our communities with gun violence and decay**

### *Stand and be accountable:*

**It is time to teach our youth how to uplift, love, and respect each other.  To value Umoj (unity), and UJIMA (collective work and responsibility) to build up our families and communities together.**

### *You helped teach them how to kill and to die*

# <u>Now teach them how to live</u>

**<u>To excel, and value each other's lives.  Teach them how to become solid Family Men,  Entrepreneurs of legitimate businesses, or to embrace Emerging Business Opportunities on a  Global Scale</u>**

### <u>Teach them how to live as real men</u>

Those of you in our community who have earned millions and millions off spewing negativity into the minds of our young men and women.  You have a responsibility to step in and step up to make massive constructive changes.   Change the messages to one of self-empowerment, self-development, self-worth, and self-sustainability.

Again, cause and effect is absolute in the Universe.  What ye sow, sow shall ye reap.  It may not be in this generation, but you and yours will pay sooner or later for what has been done by us to the last three or four generations of A-A youth.

> *African American on African American Crime:*
> *for they are swift to shed blood. How useless*
> *to spread a net where every bird can see it.*
> *These men lie in wait for their own blood; they*
> *ambush only themselves!!*
> *Proverbs 16, 17, 18.*

## 16. *Escapism.*

Over many years and throughout our communities, many of us have engaged in wholesale escapism often engaging in mind altering or mind-numbing substances and associated activities while living lives of desperation.  Escapism is a false reality but sooner or later your mind comes back to your reality. And there you are, back where you started or worse, not to mention the lives you destroy by your actions.   The secret is to do what is wise and prudent to change your reality to one of self-sustainability and service.

> **"Cast down your bucket where you are."**
>
> Booker T. Washington

## 17. *Minimal Focus on Community-based Economic Infrastructure.*

We are the biggest consumers in the economy and the least producers.  This must stop. Every culture comes and sets up shop in our communities and we self-insultingly spend our money that they take back to their communities.  Their children are not in our schools.

Many who set up shop in our communities, overcharge us and ridicule us.  They gladly take our money but have no respect for us or our community. Daily, many of us repeatedly hand our money over to someone who does not look like us, speak like us, or even respect us. They use our spending power to uplift their families in their neighborhoods.  We cannot blame them; they are merely our mirror reflecting to us our weak economic infrastructure and our weak and ungodly acquiescence to allow every culture that enters this country to get wealthy off our neighborhoods.  By comparison, Chinese, West Indians, Latinos, and others own the stores, motels, service stations, and shops in their communities and they trade with each other.  We should  feel small handing our money to another culture, often recently from another country, right in your own neighborhood when we have been living in this country semi-free for over 150 years since 1865?  No hard feelings against others for taking advantage of economic opportunities in this country.  They accomplish much by working together, investing together, working hard, and becoming prosperous together; while all too often we skin and grin, while making excuses, killing each other, and jeopardizing our future with self-hatred and mental slavery.

Just looking over the last 50 years, many of our people have made big money especially in sports and  entertainment.  Many of us spend our wealth or success on cars, homes, bling, champagne, and sometimes illicit mind-altering substances instead of contributing to building sustainable economic and academic infrastructures in our communities.

Then again, why is it so necessary for us to openly show the world that we have money with ostentatious displays?  Or bring to market outrageously expensive items that our people

cannot afford, leading to misguided values, more crime and neglected children as the "barely head above water, seek funds by any means to acquire the latest expensive but, in the scheme of things,  insignificant items that often do not contribute to sustainable economic infrastructure in our communities for the long haul.

Surely, many franchises or enterprises could have been formed and undertaken to encourage local ownership of small stores, shops, motels, gas stations, etc.   While some have invested to provide wholesome jobs and educational opportunities in our communities, more must take a page out of the Greenwood District Black Wall Street playbook.

Angela Davis

**"We must always attempt to lift as we climb"**

A major underpinning of sound economic infrastructure is financial savings.  We must respect, appreciate, and use money or the medium of exchange wisely and save, save, save. People with money do not go around boasting and showing off.  Such actions indicate you are  not appreciative, have no respect for money, and  may not have it for many generations. Have you ever noticed how people with real money always cry broke?

Further, we can be encouraged by examples of the entrepreneur spirit embraced by the West Indian, Chinese, and Hispanic Americans.  They invest in their communities and own many of the local establishments that service the local market.   Their fellow countrymen seek out their own to do business.

### 18.  *Properly Maintain Clean Environments.*

Thanks to all of you who display pride and dignity in where you abode.  But we know that sometimes, there is a failure to maintain and keep where we live clean, free of litter and rot, and often we turn where we live into litter, decay, and crime infestation.  While this is not true of all A-A neighborhoods, it really should not be true of any.  Let us get together and clean up where we live and henceforth respect our environments and surroundings.  Stop embracing the "Pig Sty Model," implanted in your head during slavery.

The dire living conditions in many of our communities today directly reflects the collective life condition of the people living there.  Lives bumbling around in the lower life conditions (hell, anger, self-destruction, apathy) attract more misery in kind for every action generates a force of energy that is returned to us in kind.  What we sow so shall we reap.  Let us expand our contribution to the happiness of humanity and produce genuine value in our communities to attract more positive and wholesome conditions.

*Remember you are what you think, you are what you eat. Artificially processed and sugary foods are low energy and unhealthy.*

19. *Failure to Stay Connected to Higher Energy Fields (Positive Vibration) of this Universe and Engaging our Third Eye.*

We must create harmony with higher vibrations in this universe through meditation: prayer, chanting, yoga, etc. We must move away from low energy fields. We must avoid such low energy fields as processed foods, excessive toxic drugs and alcohol consumption, violent behavior, profane and poor language usage, idleness, poor parenting, self-doubt, dependency, lack of self-respect, and backstabbing your own people.

The time has come to OPEN YOUR EYES to our **truth** which is too many of us are suffering from *mental slavery* as a residual effect of the Stockholm Syndrome reinforced for over 13 generations (246 years) of human bondage, depraved sexual violence, and domestic terrorism followed by another 150 years of struggling against roadblocks designed to deny our full citizenship and rights under the Constitution. While at the same time, being asked or forced to fight and perhaps die for the very country that, to this day, still refuses to fully extend democracy to the A-A people. A country where A-A communities are under siege by outsiders who ensure deliberate and easy access to guns and drugs, engage in prolific racial profiling, harasses citizens, murder them at will, and populate jails in perpetuity often because of miscarriages of justice, then go home to their suburban communities feeling gleeful about their contribution to the continued destruction of the A-A people.

The self-hatred programming was endured for hundreds of years is so deeply seated that we continue to exacerbate rather than correct. In other words, we make such awful negative causes and choices, and because of karmic retribution we undermine ourselves and attract into our communities' unnecessary multitudes of negativity and destruction. The Law of Cause and

Effect is absolute.  We must collectively begin to make better causes and choices which will, in turn, attract more  positives effects from the environment.  The place to begin is to stop killing each other without reservation. **Our lives must matter to us first.**  If we kill each other (cause) the (effect) is to help provide those outside of our community with the flimsiest of excuses to kill us for whatever nonsense they can conjure up, and not to respect and place value on our lives as fellow humans.  We must respect our lives first.

In our community, it is innocents that pay the ultimate price when our right to life, liberty, and or due process is not respected by those patrolling/occupying like  Emitt Till, Trayvon Martin, LaQuan McDonald, Sandra Bland, and countless others.  These are the ones we are aware of. Imagine how many just went missing, were found dead, or simply disappeared without ever finding accountability for the culprit(s).

A form  of panopticon has always existed in our communities.   Most often enforced by outside occupiers who feel emboldened to disrespect our lives and place little value on our self-worth. With such a myriad of evils  and wickedness coming at us from others who have shown their true colors for hundreds of years, it makes even  less sense  for us to self-destruct by inflicting devastating life choices against each other and in detriment to our own communities; imbued with such atrocities that leave the world  to wonder.  Creating generation after  generation of too many who  continue the cycle of self-destruction.    **It is simply Slavery by Another Name which is Slavery just the same.**

# Slavery by Another Name

(I dare someone to drop the microphone on this one)
By LCookHamilton

Slavery by another name
Is slavery just the same,
Now, being caught in the well woven net,
Foolishly thriving on being the jail house pet,
A source of cheap labor for "the man" like in the days of yore,
Slave shackled as they throw you in the gallows,
Then methodically disenfranchised, silencing your vote,
They calculate that you will go bragging and telling,
Priding yourself on being a felon,
Then returning to jail to be shackled again,
You need to check yourself mental slave,
Repeatedly heading to jail or an early grave.

By making bad choices you get caught in the net,
Which replaced the white sheets
But you have not figured that out yet,
Too busy self-destructing and *spouting evil* against your own,
While "the man" controls your mind,
And gleefully meads out your time,
He methodically planned to get his slaves back,
That is why he bought your soul cheap with crack,
Propelling you to steal, burn, and destroy your own community,
You need to stop this insanity,
You have a pure slave mentality,
Check yourself before we implode,
Thereby reaching the man's well-orchestrated goals.

You sell your soul cheap for a cheap ride
In a fancy car, clothes, sneakers, champagne, and a polluted mind,
While "the man" watches and laughs as you destroy your own kind,
Being controlled by some colors,

Which is a deceptive and inhuman way to get you to kill brothers,
Without forethought of the families destroyed,
You prey like an animal, mental slave
Taking out your own brothers to an early grave.

Thus, the man no longer must come in the night,
Draped in the hooded sheet with cross burning bright,
He figured it out, just give you some colors
And you will do the job for him, you will kill your own brothers.

Now look at that slave
Cannot even look you in the eye
Nothing between the ears because he did not apply,
Now you insult me when you speak,
Talking about "you know," "you know what I am saying,"
You forgot to study, so busy playing games,
So busy playing games but cannot read
Only studied sports
Now you come up lame,
Now you come up lame,
No command of the language,
Well get this!
"No, I don't know what you are saying, and stop asking me,"
As soon as you open your mouth, everyone can see
That you are a slave, men tall y.

Living without dignity, honor, or self-respect,
Mind so reduced, you do not even know,
That the body has a waistline
Cause that is where the waist of pants goes,
And not down near your toe.

Are you a parasite, a leech, selling out your community for cheap?
Leading another generation to defeat,
Look at that slave

Making babies without grace; but rave,
As if he still lives in a cave,
Makes nasty lyrics about his Momma and Sistah
Debasing women as if he will never  have a daughter
Look, or better yet, run from that  slave,
Acting as if he still lives in a cave,
As if he still lives in a cave.

You need to stop pimping your children to "the man,"
Destroying their souls by your very hands,
When you sign for a crazy check,
You make them automatic rejects,
Are you just stupid or is your mind wreaked?
Leading them to slaughter for a check.
You will be dealt with in the by and by,
For pimping your children
To the sheet hooded fox ever so sly,
Its' enough to make me cry,
It is enough to make me cry.

You sell your community out to the man,
Running to tell him everything you can,
Skinning and grinning and pimping yourself,
You stupidly think because you run and tell,
The "man" sees you differently from everyone else,
Well get this, what he sees is a fool, who will not protect
 his own,
Then he ultimately discards you, cause your soul is wrong.

Listen fool, it is time for you to make a change,
Making wise choices is the name of the real game,
Stand in the mirror for an exceptionally long time,
Look deep into your eyeballs in search of your mind,
Get close to your Divine,
And stop wasting time,

Time you do not have cause this life is short,
Take control of your life, **work**, ***read, study, and vote,***
Make our communities and children drug free,
Get back to **mothers and fathers** raising children naturally,
Seek truth and never kill or harm another brother,
**Buy from your own, that shows true colors.**

Appreciate our ancestors.  **Take your mind and hair back**,
Pushing forward is what they were about,
Stop wasting their **blood earned clout,**
**Then tell "the man" no mental slaves for sale,**
Cause I am true to my Divine,
And as a matter of fact, you go to hell,

**You go to hell !!!!!**

# Chapter 3

## No Validation is Necessary

We are the original and were not put on this planet to emulate and compliment another culture.  Each culture must define their own path. The truth is clear, we are Divinely validated, whole, and complete when we enter this Universe.  Thus, it is Divinely ordained that we do not need to be accepted or appreciated by another culture to be whole, worthy, and deserving of basic human respect and equal justice under the laws of these United States of America.

Yet, somehow since the Wicked Time, we have forgotten this truth and often seek our self-worth, evaluate what is beautiful and measure societal acceptance often in contradiction to our cultural selves which is against the rhythm of this Universe and the Laws of Nature.  Lest we forget, we descend from a mighty people, who built kingdoms and had universities long before the arrival of CI. But the underlying outcome of the deliberate mental cruelty inflicted during the Wicked Time has precipitated our perpetually chasing validation or measuring our self-worth by acceptance into the European American Group. Such misguided outreach for approval from another culture has led to misplaced values, wasted opportunities, and many unanchored children and young adults.

*Marcus Garvey*

**The Negro World Newspaper, The Universal Negro Improvement Association**

**"We must validate ourselves. We must understand that we do not need other people to tell us we are somebody… we must spend our money in our own businesses first.  We must reclaim our right to interpret our own reality and to control our own destiny."**

We keep chasing EA and they keep pulling away.  "Chasing validation is like putting your soul in a plank position" (Kanye West). When a group repeatedly compromises its dignity in pursuit of another group's norms, looks, and social acceptances; it creates an imbalance in their soul leading to self-hatred, desensitization, immoral self-destructive tendencies and actions; and tragically again this pursuit often produces ungrounded children who grow up to be angry, non-productive, non-self-sustaining adults perpetuating the cycle.

*In WW1, the 369th Colored Infantry Regiment, known as the Harlem Hell Fighters, were renowned for their bravery and skills*

Just looking at the last 150 years since the Civil War, we have sued, chased, and pleaded for acceptance and justice. I have heard speaker after speaker, pundit after pundit, politician after politician, leader after leader, minister after minster; push mantras such as, "We're in this together, black and white together," etc.  They truly believed that respect for the human dignity of all people would prevail because the United States is the purported, "Shining City on a Hill," exemplifying the standard for democracy around the universe and even invaded other sovereign nation(s) to "spread democracy." This unbridled confidence shown by our "leaders" in the willingness of those controlling the reins of power encapsulated by purported Christianity, to respect and extend to all basic decency, humanity, civil rights, equal justice and to love all like the Prophets demanded, has led to systemic injustices, sufferings, and disappointments in the A-A community and zealous pushbacks on the part of European Americans.

U.S. history confirms that time and time again, we have acted in good faith to show our deserving of being treated fairly and extended true equal rights and citizenship.  Remember, the Harlem Hell Fighters along with other brave A-A Soldiers of the Greatest Generation that defended the United States in World War I.  Seeking validation, they convinced themselves and their fellow A-A countrymen that their courageous service in helping achieve victory over dictators abroad would correspondingly achieve victory over racism at home.  They believed in the "Double V," victory abroad would surely lead to victory at home.  Without eyes opened they reasoned if they were excellent in service and in defense of their country, EA would finally extend to them true equal rights, equal justice under the law, and equal economic opportunities.

*Dr. Charles Drew, Scientist, Surgeon, and Inventor of a method for preserving blood plasma.  He started the blood bank.  His invention saved the lives of many service men.*

The War ended, and A-A soldiers returned home to red lined housing in the North.  Those living in the deep South had to change from the normal passenger cars to the Cattle Cars once the train reached the South.  Suffering from war wounds, untreated mental problems from combat, and broken hearts, the Greatest Generation and its Double V Outreach Initiative crashed and burned.  And still no validation as ensuing generations have watched and lived the disappointments.

*Over 5,000 A-A soldiers fought in the American Revolutionary War including Cripus Attucks who was the first to die in the Boston Massacre of 1770.*

Then there were the Tuskegee Airman.  A-A Military Aviators who fought in WWII. They flew more than 15,000 sorties in Europe and North Africa.  At the onset, there was wholesale pushback on the use of A-A pilots by the U. S. Military; thus, a segregated unit was established that proved itself to be superior

*WWII Doris "Dorie" Miller*

airmen of the 332$^{nd}$ Fighter Group nicknamed "Red Tails."  Sixty-six of these courageous and dedicated men died in defense of a country that has continued to discriminate against their scions. A country where, to this day, many in power boldly engage in ruthless tactics to block civil and voting rights and deny equal justice, fair economic opportunities, and globally competitive public education for all.

To recap, we have begged, cajoled, fought, and died in wars, sued, marched, and in some ways undermined our own cultural inheritance by repeatedly chasing acceptance and validation from EAs who will never give it.  We have wasted far too much time, money, and dignity attempting to mirror the looks, values, and lifestyles of the EA group. Often,  who we are primordially, has been tweaked to be acceptable to another culture in their eyesight.  If we would have used one percent of the billions we have spent on glued, permed, and sewn-in  fake hair to make our hairstyles look like we are of European descent, or purchasing outrageously expensive sneakers and other items we cannot afford; we could upgrade most of the schools in our neighborhoods and provide capital seed money towards business infrastructure.  The millions spent on fake nails alone could buy the stores and gas stations in our neighborhoods.



Ask yourself why and by whose standard of beauty and handsomeness do I view the world? And through my actions, what am I teaching my children about their self-worth.  In other words, are we not openly and by example teaching our children "their Divinely" constructed self is inferior and not worthy? Underscoring to them that we must go to extremes to alter our looks to compliment those of European descent and ignore our ancestry. Ask yourself, are we teaching our children to feel worthy and proud of their Divine selves.   Today, many of our children are crying out in their own way to A-A adults and begging them to stand up, show them high self-esteem, show them how to appreciate and respect themselves, to unite and take our full citizenship rights, to invest in our communities, and not spend money foolishly.   We owe this to the young and to help ward off our self-destruction, which without a course correction, is the likely outcome.

Malcolm X stated, "We have been sitting down, bowing down, and laying down for over 400 years in the Americus. I think it is time to stand up." It is time to turn the page on chasing acceptance, it is time to flip the script, and courageously view the CI/EA from the rearview mirror as we leave mental slavery, drug abuse, killing each other and move in unity to strengthen our communities based on a strong family structure, cooperative economics, productive work, quality education for our children, celebration of our Cultural Norms and Umoji (unity).

*Our kids and young adults  are not safe in their own back yards, playgrounds, or walking down streets in their neighborhoods: often profiled, frequently unjustifiably jailed for long periods, and sometimes shot down for simply being African-American. We are free, but not free.*  **This is just another form of racial terrorism, mental cruelty,  and modern subjugation, which projects  to the world that A-A lives are not to be valued.**

**Our kids must see that we value our own lives by stopping the gun violence.  You cannot ask for something  from others that we seem to not honor ourselves.**

To be true to ourselves, enduring and authentic, our sense of self-respect and self-worth must originate from within us and not from outside of us.  We cannot teach our children self-worth if we have not achieved it from within ourselves.  Seeking validation outside of ourselves undermines the very foundation necessary to build viable succeeding generations that will listen, be erudite, and develop into productive citizens.

So, if you are tired of whining, begging, chasing, and emulating another culture but still never being truly accepted in their world, why not embrace and preserve our A-A culture premised on our African cultural ethos and in honor of our African ancestors.  Then stand up,  "make good trouble," begin to raise more wholesome families,  insist on high academic standards and respectful behavior for youth, and bring self-sustainability to our communities.  If another culture is willing to sincerely engage with us, fine and we are grateful, but know that as of this moment we will no longer see EA as our standard barrier.  We stand on our own like any other culture in this country.  The irony is we do not need and have never needed your acceptance, love, or sympathy.  **We are over it !!!!**

*Zora Neal Hurston*

*Briggs V. Elliott- Summerton, SC*

*Historian, Dr. Keisha N. Blain*

*Ava  DuVernay, Writer, Director, Producer, Filmmaker*

**We come from a mighty people!**

My African-American brothers and sisters know this, we do not need another culture to embrace our value as humans for we have that innate ability naturally within ourselves.  It is Divine for us to look like and value our natural selves.  Henceforth, we turn our focus internally embracing self-appreciation and self-determination, and no longer labor on gaining acceptance and respect from EAs.  When we encounter them, look him/her straight in the eye and think to yourself "I do not need your acceptance, **or want it for that matter**.  Seeking your validation of our people is an insult."  Turn your head and walk away, refocus your energies within the A-A community.  Let us refocus our energies and respect on ourselves, our beautiful, handsome, divinely validated selves, because it is impossible to change the heart of people consumed with maintaining power at any cost.  No act of inhumanity is off limits when   charlatans expound religious faith from their lips yet bamboozle the people.

No more wasting our energies, prayers, and efforts trying to be loved and accepted by EAs.  We have never needed their approval or acceptance in any sphere.  We must not waste another moment **seeking their validation**.  We must use the ballot box, education, building economic infrastructures and self-sustainability to demand what we deserve.  We must begin by embracing Umoja, Kugichagulia, Ujamma, and fulfilling our Civic responsibilities.  As Nelson Mandela said, "Who are we not to be great."

<table>
<tr><td>They Came Before the Mayflower by Lerone Bennett, Jr.</td></tr>
</table>

# Like Me?

By L.CookHamilton

I do not need for you to like me,

I do not need for you to care,

In my case with your history, genuine caring would

be rare!!!


Yet, I will not allow you to discount and disrespect me,

And impinge on my citizenship rights any longer,

For today I stand stronger.


I refuse to watch you raise your hand and swear,

To uphold the Constitution and then never declare,

Truth, justice, and fairness for all.

Just engineering more strategies to ensure my fall.


Delivering more mendacity, twisted actions, and deceit,

Guess what, your time as orchestrator of my demise has been reached.

I will see you at the Ballot Box and engineer your defeat.

## A Letter to A-As from the Colonial Imperialists

By lcookhamilton

Get over it!!! I am never going to love you
For heaven sakes, I enslaved you for over 200 years
Despite your tears.
I reason that to love and accept you means my demise
For my genetics cannot overcome your melanin's power
Watching you self-destruct is my finest hour.


Every offspring increases your numbers
Potential voters you know; heck my control of the country could crumble.
Injustice, I apply at every turn
Leaving your family and community in ruins.
As I marvel with glee
I would rather see hell than respect your humanity
You had better embrace your own dignity and learn to respect
 yourself without me.


I have used black codes, lynching, Jim Crow, race baiting, vagrancy, lynching,
supplying illegal guns and drugs, injustice in sentencing, community under
occupation, racial profiling, public education by zip code, redlining, welfare,
most egregious substandard public schools, along with other tools in my war chest.

You had better realize, these tools were developed by wickedness at its best.
Steadfastly hindering you from Procreating fills me with zest
Do not fret now and you better not rest
Or I will achieve *my goal of your genocide.*

# Inauguration Day 2009

*By lcookhamilton*

Acting on Divine intervention

And with the best of intentions

You had the courage to step off the "Plantation"

*To try and bring healing to the Nation.*

During your entire Presidency, I will act insidiously

Setting up roadblocks the likes of which you will be

amazed to see.   I will never let you just be.

I will operate roadblocks at every turn

Even steal your Supreme Court placement with wicked pride

You could never have envisioned such a bumpy ride

Your people had better not dawdle or fail to vote

Else I will forever squash your idea of HOPE:

**H=help,   O=our,   P=people,   E=emerge**

# Chapter 4

## Negative Population Growth

It is all about the numbers.  Everything, and I mean everything, concerning politics, injustice, the Justice system, protecting the unborn, prison industrial complex,  the Supreme Courts and so called "our values" is about the Population Growth Numbers (PGN) in this country. Here in the United States of America, there is an on-going, underlying Civil War – **The Population Numbers War (PNW)** whose sole purpose is to make sure the A-A population numbers do not far exceed what they were at the end of the Civil War, 13%, and if possible, engineer a severe reduction.

This war is being waged against the A-A people every day and every hour. Why, you may ask? Well, it is simple.  Less people reaching adulthood, or a high percentage being locked away to serve as salve labor in the prison industrial complex, means less voters at the voting booth.  It is all about control of the purse strings and writing the history books so the actual truth will never be told.  Votes elect those that control the local, state and federal budgets, Supreme Courts and Federal Judgeship appointments; how and where monies are allocated on military spending, infrastructure development, public education, earned retirements; dependable, affordable,  and humane healthcare and childcare, etc.  Here is where the priorities of the country are determined and whether justice will be administered fairly and according to the mandates  of the Constitution of the United States of America.  The most votes control the country,  the money, and dictates its priorities; then populates the pool from which corporate boards of directors are selected and major political appointments are filled.

Let us be clear, in the 1870 Census, A-A was 12.1 percent of the population.  In 1880, we were 13.1 percent.  Transport to 2010 where we were only 13. 6 percent.  Compare to the Latino population who in 1880 were four percent and in 2010 were 16.1 percent and slated to become the majority population by 2050.  This is because they have strong family structures where men are men in the family, their own language, they do not feed on (crab-mentality) and kill each other stupidly, and they are not the biggest spenders outside of their communities. Further they own many of the business in their communities and they support those businesses.  They are incredibly careful about the cultural complement of the content delivery of Spanish networks and radio stations that feed cultural norms to their children.  The Latino community understands that if you are not the majority owner, you must observe extreme caution regarding the messaging priorities established by the fox in the hen house.  They recognize that the owners' priorities or preferred cultural depictions may or may not serve the best interest of their people.

The PGW has been executed with precision and success beyond what European America could have ever expected because of our willingness to self-destruct.  Open your eyes to the truth.  The next page clearly confirms with data that we are in a war for our very survival and must mount a more sustained, united, and strategic strategy to win.  First, we must stop killing each other with guns, substance abuse including alcohol and cigarettes, and absentee fathers.

# African American Population Growth Since 1870
## (U. S. Census)

| Census Year | % African-American | % White | % Latino * |
|---|---|---|---|
| 2010<br>308,745,538 | 13.6 | 74.8 | 16.3 |
| 2000<br>281,421,906 | 12.9 | 77.1 | 12.5 |
| 1990<br>248,709,813 | 12.1 | 80.3 | 9.0 |
| 1980<br>226,545,805 | 11.7 | 83.1 | 6.4 |
| 1970<br>203,211,926 | 11.1 | 87.5 | N/A<br>Negligible |
| 1960<br>179,323,175 | 10.6 | 88.8 | N/A<br>Negligible |
| 1950<br>150,697,361 | 10.0 | 89.5 | 1.4 |
| 1940<br>131,669,275 | 9.8 | 89.8 | 1.4 |
| 1930<br>122,775,046 | 9.7 | 89.8 | N/A |
| 1920<br>105,710,620 | 9.9 | 89.7 | N/A |
| 1910<br>91,972,266 | 10.7 | 88.9 | N/A |
| 1900<br>75,994,575 | 11.6 | 87.9 | N/A |
| 1890<br>62,947,714 | 11.9 | 87.5 | N/A |
| 1880<br>50,155,783 | 13.1 | 86.5 | N/A |
| 1870<br>38,558,371 | 12.7 | 87.1 | N/A |

*Latinos are not self-destructing by killing each other without reservation, being enslaved to the Prison Industrial Complex, fodder for the jail, or sending each other to an early grave.  *What dire self-defeatism we have engaged these days.*  It is time to **open our eyes to our truth** and free our minds of embedded self-hatred lest we self-destruct

# Chapter 5

## Population Numbers War Strategies

### (Embedded, Covert, and Overt)

To wage any war effectively, well thought out strategies must be developed and executed with animus and disdain.  Think about the ones below that have so obviously been used successfully and effectively against us.  You see the main strategy is to undermine, deceive, poorly educate, keep us dependent on mental slavery handouts, living in crime ridden communities under daily occupation, and most importantly to minimize procreation.  They keep the stage set for feeding on each other in a cycle of self-destruction and missed opportunities. Then, under overt occupation of our communities, they gleefully watch from their Country Clubs, segregated schools and communities, as they enjoy major tax breaks on the backs of the Middle Class and the poor, and aggressively try to deny reasonable health insurance  and childcare to the hard working citizens of this Country.

The chart below identifies some of the *War Strategies* in use to marginalize, undermine, dehumanize, harass, and resultantly suppress our population numbers since 1867. **War Strategies** are systemically and methodically embedded in our daily lives, while some or covertly applied or done in secret, and still others or blatantly overt that is "in your face" without conscious, religion, or humanity.

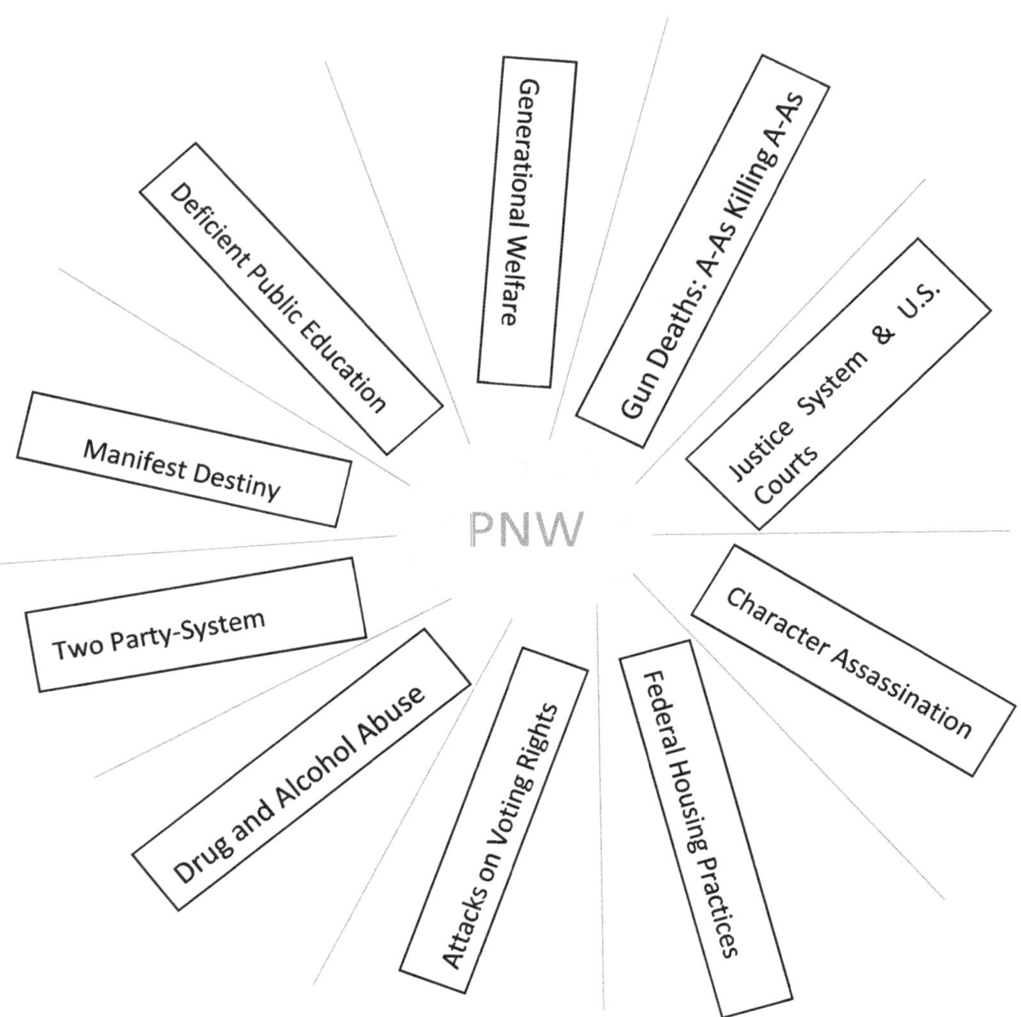


The Population Numbers War resembles a wheel. The pokes on this wheel **(PNW)** keeps the strategies on the wheel in perpetual motion against the A-A people day and night. Never letting up. ***Open your eyes and see what is in motion against us.*** The pitiful realization is that we execute much of this against ourselves because of embedded mental slavery.  See this truth and begin to make the immediate course corrections in our individual  life and teach others to do the same.

These anti-procreation and anti-A-A survival strategies are executed in a concerted and underlying Master Plan which is to dilute the voting strength of the A-A community in the Diaspora by suppressing its population numbers and ultimately engender self-destruction .

**Massive Incarcerations of A-As orchestrated by an insidious In-Justice system.  Premise on deliberate coerced, often wrongful convictions and incarcerations; and mandatory sentencing guidelines that are the 21 and 22nd$^{st}$ centuries slave auction.** According to the United States Constitution, legal slavery is only allowed after the commission of a felony which allows for civil and voting rights to be taken away.  So, by  using masked intentions like three strikes you are out, broken glass, stop and frisk, racism in drug sentencing, etc.  Jails and prisons are  the 21$^{st}$ Century Slave Ships.  A-A are inhumanely cramped in these facilities like the way our ancestors were on the slave ships.  Management can ignore occupancy standards and respect for human decency.  The underlying wickedness of it all is all too often AA men are unduly incarcerated, using trumped up charges, planted evidence, withheld evidence, racial profiling, are simply targeted as part of institutionalized oppression and 21$^{st}$ century Black Codes.  African Americans are  usually under occupation in  their own communities.  We say No More!!!

As incarceration strips one of his/her voting rights, it silences your voice. And once time is served, reinstatement of voting rights is not automatic in many states.  Further, long-term incarceration severely inhibits the opportunities of the A-A male to procreate thereby further depressing population growth.   That is why we see such well-orchestrated means to keep A-A men locked-up.  It diminishes the current and future voting power of our people.  As stated earlier, it is through the voting booth that lawmakers are chosen; the same lawmakers who determine where and how monies are spent, write and pass laws (Congress and state legislatures), fund  the military and education initiatives.  Through **voting** we elect law enforcement (sheriffs, chiefs, some attorney generals), school boards, and of course elect the President of these United States. Every person whose voting rights are taken away silences their voice as an active  participant in who makes the rules that governs them including whether justice is dispensed equally, and whether their children will have access to quality schools.

***Disparity in Drug Sentencing and failure to uphold the VI Amendment to the Constitution*** *of the United States, along with* broken class accompanied with daily racial profiling are the methods used to incarcerate A-A particularly men and boys. *Violations of the VI Amendment* causes many A-As to linger in local jails not convicted of a crime.  Constitutional Amendment VI demands "In all criminal prosecutions, the accused shall enjoy the right to a **speedy and public trial, by an impartial jury** of the State and district wherein the crime shall have been committed."  When the In-Justice system lingers an A-A citizen in jail awaiting trial often for two and sometimes more than three years, his/her voting rights are taken away and he/she loses valuable time with family often leaving behind small children, even though there has been no trial or guilty verdict rendered. Six months is excessive for a citizen to linger in jail without being convicted of a crime. Why the group responsible for making the laws, the U. S. Congress, does not mandate the Constitution be upheld always, especially since these United States of America touts itself around the world as *the beacon of Democratic values shinning on a hill*.  Once again, the hypocrisy and blatant racism without conscious can only be attributed to the PNW.

***Three strikes you are out***. Around 1994, the infamous Anti-Violent Crime Initiative with a drug possession component gave birth to one of the most egregious threats to A-As in the history of the U. S. Allegedly, it was supposed to reduce recidivism for violent repeat offenders. But with the drug possession component being added; it became a sure way for many A-A prisoners to spend decades locked-up for minor crimes based on prosecutors and judges hiding behind the three strikes you are out form of involuntary servitude. "What constitutes a strike and the number of strikes required is not even consistent from state to state". And the inhumane amount of time you can linger in jail waiting for your Constitutional Speedy Trial is criminal in and of itself.

The effort is concerted and interlinked. Many of our men and women are murdered while supposedly either being pulled over, questioned, or arrested for circumstances that are only applied to our people; or somehow always resembling someone thought to have committed an infraction, or "gee all of your living spaces look alike, so I shot, I simply had the wrong address. Oh well." The bottom line is we end up dead, missing, or like Sandra Bland where no one has explained how she ended up dead.

> Matthew Johnson, another unarmed teen shot down.
>
> Tamir Rice, another senseless death
>
> Sarah Bland, what happened?

There are blatant examples of directed efforts to keep the percentage of the U. S. A-A population at no more than 13% or less which is about what it was after the Civil War. To ensure no growth or negative growth requires a concerted effort to diminish the number of A-As in this country, particularly the number available to procreate and see those procreations live to old age. As stated, one of the most popular and utilized strategies is through injustice perpetuated by the

**Injustice System** in conjunction with the Prison Industrial Complex.

It is true that in this Country, the alleged custodian of Democratic values; there has been the deliberate, planned (Contra) and successfully executed strategy to introduce crack cocaine in the inner cities and at the same time severely increase drug sentencing for small amounts of the drug including lifetime incarceration after three strikes, leading to skyrocketing incarceration rates and long sentences; while cocaine favored by EA get a slap on the wrist sentencing.  Such unjust and inhumane drug incarceration polices have devastated many A-A communities, families, and especially children over the last half century.

## Liberty Need Glasses

by Tupac Shakur

Excuse me but lady liberty needs glasses

And so, does Mrs. Justice by her side

Both the broads r(are) blind as bats

Stumbling through the system

Justice bumbled into Mutulu and tripping on Geronimo Pratt

But stepped right over Oliver and his partner Ronnie

Justices stubbed her big toe on Mandela

And Liberty was misquoted by the Indians

Slavery was a learning phase forgotten without a verdict

While justice is on a rampage 4 (for) endangered surviving black males

I mean really if anyone really valued life and cared about the masses

They would take em (them) both 2 (to) pen optical

And get 2 (two) pairs of glasses


Historically, massive incarcerations of A-As are not a recent phenomenon. Right after the Civil War, the Southern Planter Elites/ Reconstructionist, decided to retain its exploitative slave labor under the disguise of convict lease, loitering ordinances, absent job opportunities, black codes, no housing options, fear mongering, and brutality.  No loitering ordinances applied to those just out of slavery where they lived on plantations.  These victims did not have homes so where were they to live? Thus, ensuring they were harassed and arrested as law enforcement had the power to charge fees that knowingly could not be payed, then forcing newly Freedman into Convict Lease arrangements or DeFacto Slavery.  Convict lease forced those charged to be hired out to plantations, mines, or former slave owners/abusers.  With little food and continuous trumped up charges, many died under the brutality and starvation of Convict Lease.

Then there was the application of Black Codes, a series of laws passed by states especially throughout the South to deny human rights to newly freed A-A people and retain them in DeFacto Slavery and continue using their stolen labor to fuel the economic engine of the South and enrich the Planter Elite.  These racially cruel and exploitative measures were allowed under the Presidency of Andrew Johnson  (1865-1869) who succeeded Abraham Lincoln and gave the

South a hand off approach by the Federal Government.  Johnson was followed by Ulysses S. Grant,  and Rutherford B. Hayes.

Think about it, you were arrested for loitering while in place were stringent and deliberate suppression of employment opportunities for the newly freed. You no longer lived on the plantation so where were you to go? The only jobs available were butlers, house cleaning and raising the former abuser's children and working the farm for meager wages while having to endure subhuman and insulting treatment on the job; live under segregation on and  off the job, denied racial justice, and forced to kowtow in a dehumanizing racist world held together by fear and brutality.  There was wholesale, and inhumane denial of substantial economic opportunities to earn a sustainable living.  Many newly freed citizens became part of the Convict :Lease System in perpetuity.

Like Convict Lease, today's Prison Industrial Complex capitalizes on free labor generating major financial windfalls for State budgets and private companies.  Racial profiling and community drug infestation are the feeder strategies and is so

*Medical Apartheid*

By  Harriett Washington

perversely egregious that statistics are not maintained so the world will not see "democracy in action." It is slavery by another name which is slavery just the same, and we had better open our eyes and stop our self-defeatism by not getting caught in the well-woven net and repeatedly becoming the jail-house pet.    A relentless form of panopticon was adopted as a part of Reconstruction and is even  more enforced today.

Be mindful, since the Emancipation Proclamation, 13th, 14th and 15th Amendments to the Constitution were adopted, many clever means have been used to incarcerate A-A men, or in other words Slavery by another name is Slavery just the same. Again, legally, the only place slavery is still allowed in the United States as outlined in the Constitution is for conviction of a crime (felony).  Once convicted, all rights are taken away, including the right to vote.  Remember, the Thirteenth Amendment states  in part neither slavery nor involuntary servitude, **except as a punishment for crime** whereof the party shall have been duly convicted, shall exist within the United States, or any place subject to their jurisdiction.  See the  Thirteenth  Amendment to the United States Constitution for more details.

**Generational Welfare in the A-A Community –** Capitalistic Economics maintains that, "There is no such thing as a free lunch."  Somebody, somewhere, at some point must pay.  It is equally true the best place to find a helping hand is at the end of your own arm ensuring long term sustainability and family productivity.   Generational welfare creates a recurring cycle of dependency, single parenting, teenage parenting, angry teenagers, poor education, often crime ridden and poorly maintained living spaces, and leads many A-A into a cycle of poorly educated, non-self-sustainable adults, and little hope for their children.  Welfare should be used as a short-term solution during economic hardship such as loss of a job or death while you focus on getting on your feet.   When many generations of the same lineage are caught up in the cycle of dependency, it can become self-destructive.

Think about it, common sense dictates you are not being given this "free ride," for nothing. Over generations, it is used to mentally control you ensuring that you are destroying the opportunity for your children to experience adults in the home going to work, earning their way, or pursuing an education and training for a better job and thereby empowering themselves with dignity and self-worth.  Again, the underlying mental corruption is why many welfare mothers raise the worst kids in the school, rarely show up at school to monitor classes, even with food stamps their kids must be given free breakfast and lunch, and often show up without school supplies.  Families on the dole should raise the best kids in the school system because mothers do not have to work, but mostly this is not the case.

Generational welfare dependency in its' varied forms is rot in the A-A community and is designed to destroy family structures and family values.  It is a systematic, targeted, and deliberate effort to destroy the A-A Family Structure. We thank those mothers who have used welfare temporarily during a hardship and applied it to raise productive, self-sustaining, civic minded children.

**A-A on A-A Gun Violence and The Right to Life**

If human life is sacred and we should protect it, then all human life sacred?  Why only the unborn?  I tell you why, PNW.  If only women of color had abortions, there would be no Right to Life Movement.  We cannot pretend to care about protecting human life and sit idly by, while in some years, it is estimated over 50,000 A-A young men are murdered by guns/firearms in part because of easy access to guns each year.   Killed by guns that are made readily available in the A-A community from the outside.  Since we (A-A) do not manufacture guns or rarely own gun stores, guns are being *deliberately* made easily available in A-A communities for the sole purpose of supporting and enabling A-A on A-A murder of young A-A men as a means of population control by race.    Even so, we must stop falling prey to this insidious strategy and cease the acrimony and killing of each other.  This is mental slavery at its most dangerous and wicked level.

Be aware of the deliberate existence of digital panopticon in our communities. We are under surveillance around the clock.

If such a large segment of the population is prolife, then as you raise the banner for the unborn, you should care about the children born into poverty in crime infested neighborhoods, those in Foster Care, those being shot down in their schools, those living in poverty, those living in opioid/crack addicted homes , and those attending deficient schools; with the same zeal . as you raise the banner for the unborn. Why are these state legislatures voting on prolife matters but never include anything about the thousands upon thousands of lives being shot down in the streets in urban areas, or in children foster care, etc. Do you realize that when a child ages out of foster care, they are released and must survive, often with no real family?

Many who proclaim to protect life will gleefully get a rescue dog or cat, which is nice, but never take in a child or express concern about the young men being shot down daily. If you are prolife, you must genuinely fight for all life regardless of its age or culture. To only focus on the life inside a women's body and not provide the same level of caring after the child is born is disingenuous and tells the world what you are really executing a *strategy* in the Population Numbers War. Some maintain that if only A-A and Latino women had abortions, there would be no Right to Life Movement in this Country. It all about population numbers looking ahead 20 years.

# Waylaid

*By LCookHamilton*

I inhibit your procreation and leave it lame,

Causing your population numbers to remain the same.

Guess what, you are losing this game.

Losing your voting clout and thus your power.

I must say this is my finest hour.

While you lead your own brethren to an early grave

I clap for joy because I got you waylaid

And a Mental Slave!

# A-A Gun/Firearm Deaths 2010-2016

*(Source :Injury and Prevention Control at the Centers for Disease Control).  Not all cities and states report their data to the CDC.  When it comes to A-A Firearm Deaths, they are not mandated to do so.   The actual numbers are likely much higher.   These numbers are per 100,000 A-As living in the cities/states that reported to the CDC.*

| | |
|---|---|
| 2016 | 10,101 |
| 2015 | 9,047 |
| 2014 | 7,735 |
| 2013 | 7,797 |
| 2012 | 8,021 |
| 2011 | 7,525 |
| 2010 | 7,454 |

Dead men do not procreate.  Less A-A babies born, less A-A voters in the future.  While the access to illegal guns in A-A communities is deliberate and woefully strategic, we are the ones misguided and weak minded enough to use them to kill each other.  Truthfully, we cannot blame anyone or anything but our own Mental Slavery.  It is time to free oneself from Mental Slavery and stop the killing, stop singing about killing, stop glorifying killing, stop rhyming about killing, and start respecting and uplifting each other instead of engaging in wanton self-destruction, while the orchestrators look on with glee. *We must stop letting our minds be fed and controlled by evil. **Say to yourself "No more."***

*__African American young men: wake-up, open your eyes, free yourself from **Mental Slavery** and stop doing the bidding of others and killing your own brothers.__*

**U.S. Courts and the Justice System (in-justice).**

I overheard an elder A-A acclaim "there is no justice, *just us*." Meaning the heavy hand of justice in this country keeps its foot on the necks of those in the A-A community, arresting them for any and everything, often planting evidence and even making up things, deliberately withholding exculpatory evidence, ensuring that their voting rights are taken away and their normal path to raising a family is severely limited.  The underlying goal is to strip A-A of access to the voting booth.  Our power is in the **Vote.**

**Bryan Stevenson Equal Justice Initiative (EJI)**

**National Memorial for Peace and Justice**

**The Lynching Memorial**

**The Legacy Museum**

*All in Montgomery, Al*

Remember, after the Emancipation Proclamation, the Southern Justice System passed laws and ordinances that complimented the steadfast determination of the Confederates to implement a system that will ensure A-A's remained as close to slavery as possible thereby maintaining a cheap labor to supply the economic engine of the South, that included: No Loitering, Convict Leasing, Peonage, Black Codes, Segregation, Lynching, etc.

Fast forward to the 1990's and since where three strikes you are out has allowed a major disparity in drug sentencing leading to legal slavery and a profitable prison industrial complex. There is a disparaging use of the justice system to fine, harass, and lock up for extended periods without a trial; then having a prison record, productive employment is denied.  Couple this with a lack of funding for drugs treatments, policing of urban communities where the officers do not live and treating the residents as if they were inhabitants on a plantation using racial profiling and systematic harassment of decent law bidding families.  Little has changed since the Reconstruction of the South and the same attitudes can be found across the Country.

How often have prosecutors willfully by withholding evidence or simply seating an "all-white" jury  railroaded innocent A-A men or boys into life sentences or even death.  The same is true of investigators who often engage in inhumane beatings or worse to secure a confession even when evidence confirms differently.   Somehow evidence gets buried or not shared with the defense.  To add insult to injury, often A-A suspects are provided case overloaded and often inferior counsel.  This is simply  railroading A-As to life in prison or a death sentence.  Either way, you cannot vote and your opportunities to procreate are severely minimized.  This PNW strategy has been immensely powerful and effective for many years.

On another front in the war, methodically, the PNW strategy has attempted to discombobulate the A-A male with easy access to drugs, alcohol, daily mental anguish using police brutality, and most importantly keeping guns plentiful that are used to kill each other and innocents in the community.  For example, the intentional and deliberate introduction of crack in the A-A Community by well-placed ungodly operatives was animus at its worst.

**JoAnne Gibson Robinson, Pioneer in Civil Rights**

**Septima P. Clark, Educator, Political Organizer**

**Leah Chase, Queen of  Creole Cuisine**

The takeaway is when the A-A male or female is in jail procreation is minimized.   Early deaths or dead, he cannot procreate thus the A-A population numbers will not grow significantly from census to census. This War Strategy is still extraordinarily successful, just look at the prison population numbers, funeral parlors, and cemeteries.

As mentioned earlier, another intentional practice, which has been going on since the Wicked Time is the occupation of African-American Communities by outside forces.  Many of these occupiers return to their own communities after disrespecting the human dignity and humanity of community residents.  Too often, what continues to occur without <u>justice</u> or just consequences are the willful murder of A-A's by occupiers who are supposed to serve and protect them.

**Character Assassination**

The A-A community is nudged and encouraged to slight many of its great heroes.  Systematically and deliberate attempts that often succeed in destroying a legacy of good work often spanning a lifetime and malign and disgrace the person's character for what would never be brought to bear on someone in the EA community.  The purpose is to rid our minds and hearts of our heroes, subliminally trying to destroy our sense of value and accomplishments.   Leaving few of our own for us to look up to and admire.  This is even more true, if it is an A-A  who has or is becoming or already popular across racial lines.   You can bet, there will arise some trumped-up nonsense or charges to undermine our respect for the person and destroy them outright or come back later and  attempt to destroy them in the annuals of history.  This is a Twenty-first Century Lynching and have propelled many of our greats to die early deaths denying the world more of their genius contributions.

Even in death, public lynching's continue to bash the reputations of our people even when Courts have declared the person innocent.  We must choose our own heroes and not let others dictate who we accept, honor, and admire.  We must think before we immediately assume what

*"We must recognize and defeat evil functions for they are instigated or goaded at us every day in every way"*

*L.CookHamilton*

is being presented is true.  Never immediately jump on the band wagon when the war strategy is executed to discredit and undermine the great work of one of our own.   Often, much of the purported mess is unfounded and deliberately maligning.  To be clear, just because something is labeled  "A Documentary"  in no way form or fashion proves it is true.  Always, look behind for the ulterior motives. We, unlike other cultures, are quick to undermine, ridicule, and bash our own.  Often when the person under negative review is A-A, they push one of  us out front to lead the way, skinning, and grinning (this really disappoints me) for self-gain.  Always look behind the out-front face and identify the puppeteers and their sinister motives.  Much misinformation and character assignation are hurled at our people especially those that are experiencing a modicum of success.   Know this and do not be quick to believe what is put before you.

A prime example is the Black Panther Party for Self Defense who were made to look like a violent criminal group with many of us joining the drumbeat to ridicule and label them.  But the truth is they were about men being genuine men in the community,  teaching our people to stand on their own two feet and embrace self-sustainability.  They were about education, helping the elderly with transportation, taking care of the youth in the community, and delivering nutritious food to urban areas where food apartheid existed.   Yet, they were framed, hunted down, some murdered, others jailed, while the very community they were trying to help stood idly by, even some jumping on the bandwagon and ostracizing .

Surely you realize that with advanced technology employed by groups like the Central Intelligence Agency (CIA), Federal Bureau of Investigations (FBI), Secret Intelligence Service (MI6), etc., any situation can be doctored to make the outcome appear as desired or as needed to serve the intention.  That is why we must not take these things at face value.  Because someone puts together a documentary does not make the content true.   Stop being gullible and our own must stop running out before the media to condemn our own .   Other cultures do not fall prey to this trap.   We can have deep conversations within our community.

Further, there is a deliberate, on-going, and relentless war initiative to undermine and demean the A-A Male at every turn.  Some examples: Strange Fruits, 1945 Welfare Act which in effect extended institutional dependency while removing the father figure from the home making the woman the central figure in the home.  This practice is against nature unless caused by death.  Other sinister efforts include the Tuskegee Syphilis Study, Tulsa "Black Wall Street," Disparaging in Drug Sentencing between A-A and EA, Plantation style policing of African American Communities by outsiders who sometimes deliberately target A-A men and boys for the Criminal Justice System, or sometimes murder them in cold blood.     The flood of handguns in A-A communities and the minimal sentencing when the victim and the perpetrator are both A-As are intertwined to nudge and destroy.

As a matter of fact, in urban areas, police and District Attorneys should live in the communities they serve.  If the area is not safe enough for you and your family, then it is questionable whether you will adequately protect me and my family.

Let us not forget:   some commercials, some award shows, and other media events overwhelmingly  and repeatedly present A-A's in a light  that <u>they anticipate</u> tells the world we have few solid men in the A-A community.  Notice how other cultures are not repeatedly marched out before the world to exaggerate themselves before their youth.  Yet many of us go along with it "skinning and grinning."

**Federal Housing Practices**

The National Housing Act of 1934 whose implementation arm was the Federal Housing Administration (FHA) openly allowed redlining or denying approval of mortgages to A-A based on the ethnic make-up of neighborhoods.  Steering people into segregated neighborhoods or projects ensured that neighborhoods would remain segregated with A-A neighborhoods underfunded and schools' inferior.   The Fair Housing Act (Title VIII of the Civil Rights Act of 1968) was touted to prevent a seller or renter from refusing an applicant based on race, religion, etc.   But it was never enforced.   The redlining continued unabated for generations. Industry relocated to the suburbs (white flight) leaving the urban areas depleted of economic infrastructure leading to subsidized housing often in densely populated projects, generational welfare, absentee fathers, underfunded public schools, and daily racial profiling by law enforcement who live in the suburbs.  The so called "white flight" was encouraged and financing made available to support said families flight to the suburbs and companies relocating in kind.  Of course, society came upon a new term for communities being deliberately left in distress "ghetto."

> **Senator,** Hiram R. Revels
> **Senator,** Blanche K.  Bruce
> **Senator** Edward W. Brook III
> **Senator,** Carol Moseley-Braun
> **Senator** Barack Obama
>
> **Congressman** Jefferson F. Long
> **Congressman** Joseph H. Rainey
> **Congressman,** John Lewis
>     Civil &Voting Rights Icon
> **Congresswoman** Shirley Chisholm, Presidential Candidate in 1972
> **Congresswoman** Barbara Jordan, Nixon House Judiciary Committee
> **Congressman** Elijah Cummings
> **Congressman** Adam Clayton Powell, Jr.
> **Congressman** John James Conyers, Jr.
> **Congressman** Kweisi Mfume
> **Congresswoma**n Shelia Jackson Lee
> **Congresswoman**  Terrycina Sewell
> Add your choices:
> ___________________________
> ___________________________

With limited job opportunities, declining schools, and densely populated neighborhoods, the cycle of dependency became a novelty.  And it is one of the most destructive things ever introduced to us as a people.

**Blatant Attacks on Voting Rights**

There is extreme gerrymandering combined with other state and local laws to hinder rather than encourage voting.  Imagine the United States, this alleged example of Democracy to the world,  refuses to make voting easy and convenient such that as many people as possible vote. For example, voting should be allowed on weekends when most citizens are not working.  Why schedule voting on a Tuesday when much of the Country is focused on getting to and from work, assisting and reviewing homework, getting dinner, etc.?  You should be able to choose Saturday or Sunday to go to the polls and exercise your Constitutional duty or so  by mail-in, or online.  As a matter of fact, why not allow voting on Saturday, Sunday, and Monday.  This will make it convenient for weekend workers as well.  Then there is the relocation or closing of polling places to increase the distance many A-As must travel to cast their votes, and other shenanigans.  There is nothing off limits when it comes to keeping people of color from voting.  It has always been so throughout the history of this "democracy."

**Drug and Alcohol Abuse**

Many A-A men, women, and teenagers have sought escapism from our grueling day to day struggles to survive occupation and being denied full citizenship rights and other mental health issues that go untreated.  For some, it is easier to access mind-altering substances that have been deliberately placed in our communities, than to access constructive treatments and counseling.

The bottom line is, we must decide to look evil in the eye when it appears and say "NO".  Evil acts and actions spouting from the hearts of those attempting to maintain control and marginalize us will never cease to appear in our communities.

**Two-party System**

My father Joel Hamilton told me repeatedly growing up, "Democratic Party or Republican Party, for the A-A, the outcome is the same.  One Party stabs you in the back, the other Party stabs you in the front.  Either way you are dead…."  The Constitution does not establish Political Parties as the foundation for government in the United States.  This system stifles emerging, futuristic and independent thinkers; and engenders cookie-cutter rhetoric, talking points,  and a bamboozled public.  Perhaps it is time to rethink this matter.  At one time, there was the "Liberty Party," and of course the Independent Movement.   Further the two-party system has led the country to extreme gerrymandering, voter suppression of many kinds, dog whistle politics, bamboozling a certain middle class; **and massive obscene** money and its undue influence controlling the Executive and Legislative arms of national and state governments.

Imagine a news media that identifies elected officials as Public Servants rather than tagging the person with a party label, which from the outset of a conversation, puts the person in a certain box and the effect is some voters will immediately tune out.  Politicians are public servants  and should be referred to as such.  Forget a Party label .  If we allow them to serve as public servants instead of being  a talking head for Party talking points, we will attract amazing talent, authenticity, and earth shadowing ideas into the public sphere for the betterment of all humanity.

**Manifest Destiny**

The belief that those of European descent are destined and ordered by Devine Spirit to rule over peoples and nations. Because it is my destiny, I will invade your sovereign land, kill, rape, pillage, (ask the Native Americans, Hawaiians, and today Iraq, Syria, Libya, and others),  by deploying U.S. military power to destabilize and rule your country which naturally unleashes systemic hate towards Americans that simmers and, over time, has adverse consequences in the land of Democratic Values.  Manifest destiny along with the excuse of Spreading Democracy, is the justification for having slaughtered millions in the past while pretending to embrace Christianity.  Then threaten to bomb any nation that dares to say, "respect my sovereignty" the same as you want yours respected.  Military power does not make a country the ruler over men or nations.  The United States has year after year, spent trillions of our tax dollars so desperately needed here at home to maintain foreign bases.  Notice few are on the Continent of Africa and here in our own back yard: South America and Mexico.  Focusing on development in our own backyard (instead of Japan, Germany, and other parts of Europe for instance) would have more than likely prevented the need for the hysteria over migration today.

**Systematic and Deliberate Access to Substandard Public Education and  limited Advanced Training**

Throughout slavery, the mere desire of a slave to learn to read could get him/her killed. Imagine that, it was against the governing Black Code to teach a slave to read or for the slave to indicate the desire to learn to read.  The desire to learn came with us from the Motherland and we remained mentally astute and dreamed of the day we would be free to pursue learning.  As with most everything else, after the Civil War and the limited success of the Freedman's Bureau because its initiatives were managed by locals who had been traitors to the Union; systematically, substandard public-school offerings were put in place for A-As that are systemic across the country today.  Deliberate substandard facilities and educational opportunities are deployed in most areas where large A-A student populations attend school.  It is often referred to as ascertain the caliber of public education by the zip code.

Imagine if major players like Google, Microsoft, Hewlett Packard, Amazon, Facebook, Apple, IBM, Tesler, etc., invested in HBCU's like Howard University, Hampton Institute, Alabama State University, Florida A&M University, etc., built facilities and underwrote the education of students in disciplines as  Engineers, Cybersecurity Experts, Coders, AI Developers, E-Gamers, IT, Robotics, Cyber Transports, Doctors, Quantum Physics, Alternative Currencies,  etc. instead of importing foreigners and then complaining about theft of intellectual property.  Year after  year, you invite foreigners in instead of training your own countrymen.   It only fair that Recipients  of underwritten educations would have to agree to work for a company for four or five years to allow the company to recoup the investment.  Shame on you American Companies for not investing in your own countrymen.

*The Social Life of DNA
& Body and Soul*
By Alondra Nelson

Finally, there has always been a master plan premised on the Underlying Civil War in this country "the Population Numbers War (PNW)." As stated earlier, the winner of this war will control the vote, thereby controlling the courts especially the Supreme Court, courthouses, statehouses, House of Rep. and Senate; and the Presidency of these United States; and thus the budgets or the allocation of funds, associated priorities; and the might of the  military.

Hard Working Latinos Come to Town

While EAs were so keenly focused on depressing the population growth of A-As, they ignored the significant growth in the Latino population and their numbers are sure to eclipse EAs by no later than 2050.  Suddenly, desperate, and inhumane measures are underway.   But it is too late for the train has already left the station.  Perhaps EA can slow the train's arrival, but it will pull into the next station and Spanish will be the language of the day.  We must teach our children Spanish so they will continue to be employable in the future.  How karmic, since historically much of this land once belonged to Mexico, while some other parts were acquired from Spain who stole it from Indigenous People.

# Chapter 6

# You Cannot Legislate the Heart

Judicial Decrees, street marches, sit-in, etc. have not changed the true racial feelings harbored by people as they incessantly take actions to keep true to those feelings and pass them on to future generations.   Their true feelings are always simmering underneath. You cannot erase a person's heart.  For a time, they may push their ideology/hate/racism under the surface, but as soon as the political climate or societal environment  presents the opportunity, they will gladly step up to let the world know how they truly feel.  So *at this moment in our history, it is imperative we* open our eyes and see the underlying truth that you cannot legislate the hearts of people. We should have this figured out by now considering the many years we have overly relied on Legislation instead of overly relying on self-empowerment "You can never win an argument by getting into people's heads or by forced cooperation, you must get into their hearts." "Educating the mind without educating the heart is no education at all" said *Aristotle.  No matter how long a log stays in the water, it does not become a crocodile  (African Proverb).*

Open your eyes and know that we have not and will never penetrate hearts reinforced behind Christian hypocrisy, racism, code words, and dog whistle phrases like "protect our values,"  "Christian Values," and the general willingness of so called persons of faith to bamboozle their people. . lets' look at some of the many attempts to Legislate the Heart of the CI, and later European Americans.

Legislative Efforts over time

| Year | Judicial Ruling, or Executive Order, or Legislative Act | When Decreed | Purpose | Outcome |
|---|---|---|---|---|
| **1863** | **Emancipation Proclamation** | "all slaves in the rebellious states, "shall be then, henceforward, and forever free." | Punish the Southern States that had betrayed the Union | The Executive Order was ignored by the Confederate States. The Proclamation did not free a single slave in the South until after the Civil War |
| **1865** | **Thirteenth Amendment** | *The Amendment Thirteen* to the Constitution of the United States of America, ratified in December 1865. Neither slavery nor involuntary servitude, **except as punishment for a crime** whereof the party shall have been truly convicted, shall exist within the United States, or any place subject to their jurisdiction. | To Abolish Slavery in the U.S. | Loitering Ordinances Peonage Convict Lease Sharecropping Black Codes The deliberate suppression of critical transitional supports such as gainful employment<br><br>(simply slavery by another name) |
| **1865** | **Black Codes** | Laws pass primarily in Southern State Legislatures to legally restrict the human rights of newly freed A-As and keep their economic and civic options as close to slavery as possible. For example: employment opportunities were | To ensure a stable and subservient work force and to reinstitute slavery which included controlling the activities A-As could or could not do.  For example, A-As | Robbed A-As of their dignity and voting rights, subjected them to substandard public education and health services, and allowed for limited job opportunities beyond sharecropping. DeFacto Slavery. |

| | | | | |
|---|---|---|---|---|
| | | very scarce so A-As were forced to enter unfair and grossly underpaid labor contracts to work for the CI in agriculture, domestic servitude that included governess. | could not assemble in a group unless a CI was present. | |
| **1865** | **Freedmen's Bureau** | The Bureau of Refugees, Freedmen, and Abandoned Lands whose mandate was to provide employment, relief, housing, education, and social reconstruction for four million newly freed A-As and settle them on confiscated land from traitors. | It failed mightily in that President Andrew Johnson supported the efforts of the former Confederate States to make the South as close to pre-Civil War as possible. And the Bureau was dependent on local CI administrators who sabotaged efforts. | Inferior Public Schools and accommodations, segregation, and Jim Crow. |
| | **Remember the Sixth Amendment to the Constitution** | In all criminal prosecutions, the accused shall enjoy the right to a speedy and public trial, by an impartial jury of the State and district in wherein the crime shall have been committed... to have compulsory process for obtaining witnesses in his favor, and to have the | To ensure citizens did not linger in jails without trial. Extended to A- A when the XIII and XIV Amendments were passed. | For over 150 years, A-A have been made to linger in jails awaiting trials, evidence withheld, subjected to jury verdicts by skin color. |

| | | assistance of counsel for his defense. | | |
|---|---|---|---|---|
| **1868** | **Fourteenth Amendment** | All persons born or naturalized in the United States and subject to the jurisdiction thereof, are citizens of the United States and of the State wherein they reside.  No State shall make or enforce any law which shall abridge the privileges or immunities of citizens of the United States; nor shall nay State deprive any person of life, liberty, or property, without due process of law, nor deny to any person within its jurisdiction the equal protection of the laws. | Make it clear who are citizens of these United States and guarantee equal protection of life, liberty, and property. | Racial profiling to present day, broken glass policing, lingering in jails awaiting trial for sometimes years, often trump up charges accompanied by long jail sentences. Redlining, extreme gerrymandering, and blatant voter suppression |
| **1870** | **Fifteenth Amendment** | *The Amendment Fifteen, ratified in 1870.* The rights of citizens of the United States to vote shall not be denied or abridged by the United States or any State because race, color, or previous conditions of servitude.  Section 2. The Congress shall have the power to enforce this article by | Ensure A-A males the right to vote | Without penalty, many States employed means such as poll taxes, literacy tests, threats of violence, inability to find employment, to deny A-A the right to vote. Congress has weakly intervened with Civil Rights and Voting Rights laws instead of levying hefty fines against States that violate the fifteenth amendment.  Today, many of us are falling |

| | | appropriate legislation.<br><br>MLK stated in a 1967 Speech: The Other America.  In the final analysis, racism is evil because its ultimate logic is genocide. | | prey to the latest means of denying our voting rights and that is becoming participants of the Criminal Justice System and disrespecting our Right to Vote by not voting in every election. |
|---|---|---|---|---|
| 1920 | **Nineteenth Amendment** | The Amendment Nineteenth, ratified in 1920.  The right of the United States to vote shall not be denied or abridged by the United States or by any State because sex.  Congress shall have power to enforce this article by appropriate legislation. | Extend the right to vote to Women | European American women voted without interference.  A-A woman continued to be denied with poll taxes, literacy tests, night riders, etc. |
| 1957 | **Brown V Board of Education of Topeka Kansas** | Separate but equal is inherently unequal | Attempted to force the Federal Government to make schools equal in facilities, books, teachers, financing, and access to quality education. | Forced school integration leading to forced busing.  Many A-A schools were closed, their history lost, and A-A teachers and administrators lost their jobs. |
| 1960 | **Civil Rights Act** | Attempted to penalize poll workers who denied the vote to A-A | To remove obstacles set up to keep A-As from registering to vote | Locally not enforced |
| 1964 | **Civil Rights Act** | Outlawed employment discrimination based | To end discrimination and segregation | Plantation mentality style policing in A-A neighborhoods by |

| | | on race, and segregation in public places | in the public realm | outsiders who go home to the suburbs. Segregated communities, segregated country clubs, broken glass/plantation style policing, more private schools leading to more segregated schools, enhanced cycle of dependency, more slavery by another name (prison industrial complex and stripping away voting rights) |
| 1964 | **Twenty-Fourth Amendment** | *The Amendment Twenty-four* to the Constitution of the United States, ratified in January 1964. Section 1.  The right of citizens of the United states to vote in any primary or other election for President or Vice President, for electors for President or Vice President, or for Senator or Representative in Congress, shall not be denied or abridged by the United States or any State by reason of failure to pay any poll tax or other tax. Section 2.  The Congress shall have power to enforce this article by appropriate legislation. | To stop the overt and deliberate attempt at disenfranchisement by levying a tax on A-A attempting to register to vote. | Extreme gerrymandering designed to dilute the voting strength of minority communities. |

| 1965 | **Voting Rights Act** | To guarantee the voting rights established when the 15th Amendment was ratified. | To remove laws and barriers to vote that had been established by State and Local Governments | Gerrymandering, voter id laws, limited weekend voting across the country, denial of automatic restoration of voting rights, wholesale purging of voting rolls. |
|------|------|------|------|------|
| 2018 | Athletes must stand for the Pledge of Allegiance.  You must stand for the Pledge. | Forced to stand for the Pledge regardless of how their rights are trampled on in their Country, or losing their job, or risk incurring extreme fines, etc. | Athletics were punished for not standing, yet have been subjected to racial profiling and unrelenting harassment and community occupation,  for hundreds of years in a country where many A-As fought in wars and died in support of the Stars and Stripes | * |

***You cannot Legislate the heart.**  For example, you may take a person's livelihood away for not standing for the flag or try to shame him/her, but as A-As have experienced firsthand,  you cannot govern or legislate what is truly in the hearts of people. We have seen your heart for 400 years.  In fact **many in the United States continue to harbor ill will** in their hearts  towards us despite their descending from ancestral participation in the most wicked physical, sexual, and mental abuse, of humankind, not to mention hundreds of years of stolen labor.

**But it works both ways**.  For example, *even if I am standing for the Flag, <u>I could be saying</u>:*

"I Pledge to stand for the Flag of the United States of America

And to <u>never </u>succumb to the attempted genocide

And wickedness for which it stood over my ancestors.

And I insist the Republic will live up to ***its creed***

To give Liberty and Justice to all."

Today's Dog Whistle  political  climate encourages people to openly admit what has been true all along, and that is the underlying embracing of racial injustice and intended marginalization of the A-A in many  hearts.   From simmering just underneath the surface, it is now willingly touted and shouted.  And yet he/she sits piously on the pew every Sunday finding ways to cloak themselves in hell destined excuses for how they treat their fellowman.   Imagine that…

Since the Civil War, we have pursued an agenda that has failed to achieve true equality and equal justice under the laws as set forth under the Constitution and adopted Amendments.  Yes, Congress and State Legislatures can write and pass bills that become laws and the Supreme Court can render a verdict, but the true underlying impact on society of any law depends on the hearts of the masses.  Clearly, sustained fairmindedness and extending basic human decency and Constitutional rights to A-As has not genuinely emerged in the hearts of many in this country.  And there is clearly an embedded willingness by many to embrace religious hypocrisy, while at the same time bamboozling the middle class and poor into voting against themselves.

Historically, changes in oppressive behavior usually comes about by force often military defeat with a usurp of power like occurred in Santo Domingo and some other parts of the West Indies.  There the slaves rose-up and overthrew the CI by force and reclaimed their humanity over time.  Some other islands in the West Indies were extended civil rights and the right to govern themselves early on and quality education was made available to all.  That is why they do not suffer from the residual effects of prolonged brutal servitude as intensely as we are experiencing as A-As.  They have an entrepreneurial spirit, embrace education, and support their community businesses.

But we got bamboozled into thinking the Civil War would bring an end to our oppression and usher in true freedom, equal justice, full citizenship rights,  fair housing, quality education and job training.  It was not so, was never intended to be so, and many learned  men have gone to their graves having ushered in policies, laws, and customs that cursed the lives of the descendants of the Wicked Time, and more ingeniously, engrained in us the will to undermine and destroy ourselves from within.  **But we say NO MORE**.  Our eyes are opened and we courageously say **NO  MORE!!!!.**

**The Election of Barack Obama was Divine.**  It was so Divinely Ordained that his life was so pristine, no amount of money, investigators, investigations, the IRS, and willful, degrading slander from birthers could successfully blemish his background, academic prowess, or dignified demeanor.  *He was coveted Divinely all his life to become the Healer of the United States and move the country from hypocrisy to a true "shinning city on a hill" example for the world to emulate.*  The willful executioners of the Population Civil War controlling the Power refused to support and accept what the Universe Divinely set forth.

For this egregious crucifixion, the nation will undergo instabilities in many forms for into the future. **For racially charged and deliberately cruel reasons**, President Obama had every kind of evil known to man thrown at him, yet he never wavered in his dignity or determination to serve at his best as he rescued the economy from the abyss, lowered unemployment to a historical low, extended health insurance opportunities to all, was a great Commander in Chief,  showed respect and concern for the environment, and exampled a man/father supporting and valuing his wife and children; and gained the respect of the countries around the world.

  History will show, and the hearts of men already know, he accomplished much despite the devil personified against him.  And that swagger.  Imagine what he could have accomplished and where the country would be if he had been treated according to the teachings most in this Country claim to embrace.  But the glaring hypocrisy is almost blinding.

**So Like** Nat Turner, never forget our Drums.  We brought the beats from the Mother Land in our soul and held onto them while enduring all forms of wickedness.   Let us beat our drums and keep the wicked at bay.    **Our Eyes are Opened, we see you and your intentions.**

### John Robert Lewis

**"Never let anyone, any person, or any force dampen, dim, or diminish your light"**

Honorable U. S. Representative for over 30 years, Civil Rights Pioneer who was beaten in Selma, Alabama  on Bloody Sunday,  March 7, 1965.  He was one of the leaders of the Student Nonviolent Coordinating Committee (SNCC).

He encouraged us to "Make Good Trouble."

## Chapter 7

## *Forgiving, Seeing Clearly, Healing*

## *and Redemption*

**W**e *praise, respect, and profoundly appreciate the A-As who are being good parents,*

*economically self-supporting, raising capable and disciplined children, valuing education, demanding good manners, performing their civic duties, and being self-respecting citizens. Thank you for being wise enough to stand tall amid the genocidal war that is relentlessly waged against us and at the same time not falling prey to participation in self-defeating tendencies. We honor you and we appreciate you for your accomplishments have not been easy.  We say continue to stand tall.*

Admittedly though, this success is not being experienced or lived by a large portion of our communities.  Thus, it is imperative that we have the fortitude and unwavering confidence to acknowledge our truths, take full ownership of our shortcomings, and begin to rely on the invincibility descended to us by our ancestors and move forward with Nia and Umoja towards redemption.  Moving forward demands that we first forgive ourselves for some of the most egregious and damaging assaults on our humanity and these are the ones we have done to ourselves.

For those who have been and remain at war against us, removing crippling anger from our hearts **does not mean forgetting, excusing your crimes against humanity and blatant terrorism, or releasing you from  legal accountability.**   We forgive to  secure our own clarity and peace of mine to refocus our energies on improving our communities and taking power at the ballot box. We **chose to not let**  the mean spiritedness and wickedness you hurl at us daily, define us or tie up our insides such that we cannot see your truth and move forward in spite of it.   Lastly, to receive favor from Divine Forces, we must remove disgust from our hearts.

These are the first steps to our healing and jettison mental slavery:

*Forgive Self:* We forgive ourselves for the missteps we have committed against ourselves  since the Civil War 1865-1919:

We forgive ourselves for being willing participants in our own destruction by not recognizing and scouring the psychological and mental conditioning and its generational transmittal characteristic underpinnings that have continued to instill self-hatred and self-defeatism in our psychic, and often negatively impacts our actions in our families and communities.

We forgive ourselves, for almost destroying the A-A Family Unit in many of our communities.  For the missing fathers/husbands who should be the head of household and support the family along with a nurturing wife/mother,  and together parent obedient, respectful, and educationally focused children.  Mothers and fathers are central to the cognitive and sound emotional development of their children which contributes greatly to positive self-esteem.  It is critical for us to understand that, while not impossible, it is difficult for a woman to teach a boy how to be a man, how to treat a woman, and how to be the head of household and support a family.  In other words, we want our boys to adopt or aspire to the qualities of a genuine man.

We forgive ourselves for those unnecessarily participating in Generational Welfare and its destructive intentions.  Many of us are complicit by not understanding that there is no such thing as a free lunch.  Dependency laden welfare policies  for A-As and associated rules are specifically designed to destroy the A-A family unit and many of our people have fallen into the well woven net, and as a result, have failed to teach our children the value of working for what you need and want. On this day, at this moment, each of us should commit to building self-sustaining families.  We must never forget that hard-work and self-sustainability are two of the hallmarks of our African lineage? Self-sustainability is the hallmark to positive self-esteem, self-worth, self-respect, and self-confidence.

Rev. T. D. Jakes<br>
*"A setback is a setup for a comeback"*

Rev. Richard Allen, AME<br>
*One of the first Religious and Civil Rights leaders.*

We forgive ourselves for choosing the way of the Talented Tenth and Forced Integration instead of focusing on community-based Economic Empowerment and skills mastery.

We forgive ourselves for wanton self-insults and self-hate.  Although most difficult, we must forgive ourselves for engaging in acts supporting self-defeatism including those using the airwaves to provoke, encourage, and embolden our boys to kill and or interact with anger and animosity towards each other.  We forgive our men and teenage boys for the senseless, stupid, and cruel violence resulting in morbid self-destruction.  "Forgive him, for he knows not what he does."  Or does he?  Or is he/she simply a mercenary soldier in the Population Numbers War programmed to be mentally weak and kill his own. Ask yourself.  Again, who is really making the big money and living large on perpetuating slaughter.  Follow the money....

We forgive ourselves for those in our Communities who have engaged in excessive use of mind-altering substances of all types, both legal and illegal to sustain a polluted mine and destroying many lives including children caught in the wake.  Such behaviors riddle many of our communities with crime, violence, and physical decay while supplying free labor to the Prison Industrial Complex.

We forgive ourselves for some who have amassed felonies and now encourage others not to vote.  "Man, they are going to do what they want, so I don't vote." Never mentioning that you have lost your voting rights.  Spreading of this debilitating apathy throughout our neighborhoods is negligent and destructive.   Shame! Shame!

We forgive ourselves for often operating from a CRAB mentality towards each other.  Failing to support each other on the way up and often trying to hinder or pull the person down who is trying to be successful.  Let us agree to cease and desist with this wickedness today.  Help do not hurt.

We forgive ourselves for the truth that some of our children grow up with adverse childhood experiences causing barriers to learning leading to angry, emotionally damaged, and desensitized personalities who as adults, perpetuate living on the dole, recidivism, and another generation of poor parenting.

We forgive ourselves for allowing the slave mentally to reside and be generationally transmitted such that, for generations, we have allowed ourselves to live under occupation in many of our communities subjected to stop & frisk, broken glass, forced confessions, mandatory sentencing, three strikes, a high percentage of erroneous convictions many on death row and serving as a springboard to many District Attorneys becoming Governors, Representatives, Senators, etc.

We forgive ourselves for being distracted and gullible to spend our financial resources on nonsense and immediate gratification instead of building solid economic infrastructures in our communities.  Unlike other cultures, our money is spent in a way that sends it outside of our community.  We are exceptionally large consumers with little economic infrastructure to show for it.

We forgive those of us who have not always embraced the quest for knowledge and demanded our children be highly educated and learned as was the desire of our ancestors.  We must teach our children to become certified, credentialed, licensed, or skilled in something that affords a self-sustainable living.

We forgive ourselves for not adopting Ujamaa (Cooperative Economics) throughout our communities.  List several areas of forgiveness you identify:  ___________________ ____________________________ ____________________________.

*We mentally wash ourselves clean of these things and no longer participate in our own undermining and destruction.* NO MORE!!!!    We are grateful for this chance to grow and change.

*"NO MORE" is our Battle Cry.   And we say, "No More" because we are going to clean up our own house, become unified, and build solid economic infrastructures in our communities.  For us to move forward with clarity of purpose and Universal favor, we must forgive those who trespass against us.* We forgive to remove the inner poisons that are eating away at some of us, **but we will forever remember and hold you  morally and legally accountable for** the enduring evils perpetuated against us.  We will intentionally make special reference as we share history with our youth on our major holidays.  We commit to proudly teach our children to remember and to stand on the sacrifices and hard-fought rights secured by our ancestors; especially the right

> **The Green Book**
>
> **Henrietta Lacks (HeLa),**
> **the Mother of**
> **Modern Medicine**

to vote, right to earn a living wage, right to public accommodations, the right to have access to quality education and quality healthcare, and the right to be free of police harassment in our communities.  If you do not live within five miles of the community, you should not patrol it.  You become an occupying force that behaves like one.  Go home and patrol your own community where your children attend school, and where you spend your paycheck earned off the backs of harassing people of color. You do not spend your earnings in our community. Give these jobs to people that live in the community.

**Again,  open our lives to receive Divine favor, and thus allowing ourselves to move forward, we are obligated to extend forgiveness to our enemies but _never_ trust or forget their wicked atrocities against us during slavery and those blatantly  being executed by their descendants today (for example: making every underhanded and vile attempt to keep us from exercising**

**our right to vote, mandatory sentencing for young African American men, police occupation of communities where they do not live, substandard education, clean water, and access to quality healthcare).** **We** forgive but we will NOT FORGET or stand unguarded. **Our eyes are opened**, and we see you clearly and your perilous intentions that are outshined by our invincibility and our greatness. We will honor our ancestors and reclaim our ancestral greatness that existed for millions of years before you invaded our Motherland.

> *Our youth will remember and teach their children about the myriad of injustices, and pure evil that was done to our ancestors, and still continues in other forms today.  We will never forget the wickedness: physical brutality (scourge, mutilation, lynching, branding), mental cruelty such as selling away children, Apartheid, massive  sadistic sexual exploitation against females and males, racial terrorism, and downright disrespect of our Divine humanity.  Egregious human rights abuses including wholesale denial of equal rights, red lined housing, no living wage job opportunities leading to sharecropping, convict lease, and defacto slavery.  The deliberate and calculated efforts to keep us living the same lives as before the Civil War.*

**We** know that during the Wicked Time, you denied our ancestral languages along with education. It was even forbidden by severe beating and even death for a slave to be taught to read and write.  We can extrapolate the same is true today, "deny A-A children quality education, using their zip code." With the disgraceful conditions of public education in neighborhoods of color in this country, it is clearly a rose by another name.   Prisons are constructed in this county based on the performance of A-A children by the end of the Third Grade.  Imagine that.  That is how embedded the intended failure, using the denial of quality public education, drives how people use their votes to send people to the House of Representatives, the Senate, and the State Houses who will stand firm on the underlying mission to destroy the A-A community in this Country.

**Historically,  we have seen** countless covert and overt attempts to deny A-A Civil and Voting rights including Literacy Tests, Jim Crow Laws, and Institutionalized Segregation.   EAs, you engage in willful deceit, you even deceive yourselves with your shortsightedness.  Ask China, Japan, Russia, or India. The first line of defense of any Country is its capable people and not people you  import with many being spies against you.   How can it be wise to not fill universities with your own citizens first?   Why not make quality public education available and free in this country regardless of your zip code?  Then you can fill your universities with your own citizens.

> *While we are not going to extend animosity, we see you and your pervasive attempts at undermining us as a people including exposing us to inferior infrastructure such as polluted water, lead paint infested buildings, substandard public education; an unjust Justice System, and forever creating excuses to rob us of our right to vote including extreme gerrymandering and blatant voter suppression tactics.*

**We** know you have always encouraged the deliberate destruction of the A-A family unit, for the deliberate Food Apartheid in many Urban areas.  You structured Government handouts to promote generational dependency and destroy the A-A family unit.  We will strive for self-sustainability.

**W**e  hear EAs dog whistle politics.  We hear you.  We see your ungodly intentions.

**We** recognize the scourge and profit motive of the Prison Industrial Complex or **Slavery by Another Name** and the blatant disregard for the Fourteenth Amendment when it comes to A-As.

**We**  hold EA accountable for the blatant racial profiling that continues unabated today.   Many young men shot down, chocked, or beaten while simply existing while A-A.   Abused daily by those hired to "protect and serve" but rather work as an occupying force then go home to a different zip code, school system, tax structure.

**We** hold EA accountable for  this unholy unjust Criminal Injustice System and its Courts, and its abusive prosecutorial arm with the Constitutionally mandated <u>Speedy Trial</u> totally ignored.

**We** know you deliberately placed the most devastatingly addictive drugs in our communities. But "cause and effect" is absolute as you now see with the Opioid epidemic, what ye sow, you now reap.  We refuse to continue to allow our bodies and minds to be polluted.

**We** know EAs  flood our communities with guns enabling easy access for the sole purpose of encouraging us to kill each other.  If these guns were **used to rob and kill in EA communities at the same daily rates**, you could not pray up a gun in A-A communities and restrictions on gun ownership would sail through Congress.

**We remove anger from our hearts because it is required of us to find favor and harmony, but these things will never be forgotten or pushed to the back of our minds.   We will use them to inspire and motivate us to uplift ourselves.  We really see you.  We recognize your true intentions towards us!!!!  Our Eyes are Opened.  WE SEE YOU !!!**

# The Mind

## Twin Verses

*The mind, the mind, the mind*

*This is the beginning and the end of it all.*

*The quality of one's life depends on nothing but the mind.*

*If one's words or deeds come from an impure mind, then suffering surely follows.*

*If one's words and deeds come from a pure mind*

*Then happiness walks with him as his own shadow*

*Living only for pleasure, stuffing oneself with this or that, being lazy and undisciplined, this makes one powerless.*

*The Dhammapada*

# Chapter 8

## Self-Empowerment

## The Process to Remove Lingering Residue

No one can empower you but you.  Do not seek empowerment outside of yourself.  It must come from within.

For millions of years before the CI invasion of the Motherland, Africa, our ancestors laid a

solid foundation of invincibility, fortitude, grit, and cultural advancement as the hallmark of our people.  Henceforth, we vigorously embrace their wisdom, mental, and physical prowess.  Each of us is making an inner determination to self-transformation thereby leading to the greatness which was descended to us.

We are awesome and remarkable to have withstood the vilest, cruelest, evilest, and most intense and directed efforts to dehumanize, disrespect, and belittle a people.  To the point where we began self-destructing by turning on each other in a mayhem of self-defeatism as the perpetuators gleefully watch from their country clubs and segregated communities, smiling as they bamboozled their own middle class, and poor.  But you, our ancestors filled us with an intense lifeforce of grit, and we are still standing to begin our Transformation back to our traditional greatness.

We recognize that the universe responds in kind and thus we will become one with the rhythm of this Universe as we undergo this self-transformative process to achieve self-sustainability.   Never forget  and use the  many ungodly actions done against us in the name of Christianity as our impetus, our motivation, the ignitor, the catalyst for our unity, self-empowerment, voting with fidelity, and our achievement of self-respect and self-sustainability. We will rise like a phoenix because our eyes are now opened, and most powerful, we see and finally admit to ourselves your true intentions towards us.

The self-transformation of our people begins with individual **Self-Empowerment Process called Reclaim The Greatness of our Ancestors  (the RTGOOA)**.

For many of us, it is critical to mentally heal and individually free ourselves from the generationally transmitted shackles in our brains, to scour our minds of the toxins and poisons deliberately implanted to self-undermine and destroy.  We must unify with each other and together embrace a course correction. I extend to you a process that will ignite the path by which one can heal, become whole again, and aggressively thwart the self-inflicted, as well as, externally orchestrated destruction that is being perpetrated on our people, our communities, and especially our young. And especially the cruel and stupid things we orchestrate against our own people and communities. The **Self-Empowerment Process** mandates we scrub yourselves clean mentally and physically as we reclaim our destiny as a mighty people.

**Let us begin by agreeing and making a shared vow that we are in covenant with one another in the Diaspora to be victims no more and determine to become the masters of our fate.  We will protect our young, our culture, protect each other, and our communities- no matter what…**

**If you agree sign here** ______________________________________________________

# The A-A Self-Empowering Process consists of eight modules:

*Module 1:*       **Reconnecting with Self and Freeing the Mind**

*Module 2:*       **Build Strong Self-sustaining A-A Families**

*Module 3:*       **Uphold Civic Responsibility without Fail**

*Module 4:*       **Maintain Neat and Clean Surroundings**

*Module 5:*       **Develop and Support A-A Economic Infrastructure**

*Module 6:*       **Become Multi-lingual**

*Module 7:*       **Contribute Positively to Our Culture and Communities.**

               **Teach our History, Teach our History, Teach our History.**

*Module 8:*       **A-A Young Male Rite of Passage,**

               **A-A Young Female Cotillion,**

               **A-A Watoo Gathering**

<u>**Self-Empowering Module 1:**</u>  **Free My Mind** (FMM)

**Purpose of Module 1:** to rid infected minds of the embedded poison and pollution, self-loathing, and negativity thereby freeing your mind and validating yourself.  Below are activities I have used and found to be invigorating, mentally cleansing, and allows me to refocus when necessary. **Begin** by getting close to the mirror and look deep into your eyes in search of your very being for three minutes.  For two of those minutes, ask yourself "who am I." Who am I supposed to be?  What is my purpose? I chose to live purpose.   End with I am worthy, I am worthy, I am worthy!"

> Dick Gregory
>
> **"If you don't program your mind, it will be programmed for you"**

It could take several tries before you can stare at yourself for three minutes.  If you fail, try again the next day.

**1.  <u>Daily Assertion for Self-empowerment</u>**  Sometimes referred to as Daily Affirmation.  Please list the following on a manageable sheet or index card one item at a time. Read these assertions daily in silence or at an audible tone as part of your morning ritual.

**I am** grateful for being blessed in all things with my family, friends, community, and self.  I extend peace, love, happiness, good health, financial abundance, and good circumstances to all I interact with today.

**I am** grateful for my health and mental clarity. All the cells and systems in my body are functioning in optimal health

**I** was born whole and complete and fully embrace my greatness  and possibilities.

**I am** worthy, amazing, courageous, and confident, and lucky.

I surrender shame and forgive myself for past negative thoughts, words, and deeds. I remove all doubt, blame, and shame from my life.

I refuse to live in the four lower life conditions of hell, anger, self-destruction, and apathy. **My eyes are open**, I see clearly and repel negativity, toxic people, toxic environments, and oppressive mendacity.

I eat to live and do not live to eat, never stuffing myself with bad food; never polluting my body and mind with illicit and or licit chemicals for escapism.

I do not dawdle or procrastinate.

I will extend acts of kindness and service today without reciprocal expectation.

I commit to a lifetime of hard work, study, learning, and helping to teach our history to our young. I will become an Erudite and extend the same to my Watoos.

I am fearless. As a scion from the Motherland Africa and because of my ancestry, I have the courage of the Lion, the Majesty of the Panther, the eye of the Eagle, and the endurance of the Elephant **for I am invincible**.

*Add your own meditation or prayer here. Or you may already have a daily meditation that you embrace.*

______________________________________________________________________

______________________________________________________________________

______________________________________________________________________

When completed, breath in deeply through your nose for a five-count, sending the breath all
the way down to the bottom of your stomach.   Exhale
through your nose for a seven count.   Repeat these
breaths for three sets.  "Breathing exercises helps clear
daily clutter from the mind and allows it to focus and to
center yourself and find your inner peace.

**We will become what we
think about all day**

Dr. Wayne Dyer

2.    **Detox**    Eliminate toxins from your life: daily use of excessive drugs and alcohol,
promiscuity, toxic people, toxic circumstances, toxic environments, gluttony, obesity, negative
thoughts, mean words, and an uneducated mind. Everyday toxicities are crippling many in our
communities.  It is up to us to detox.

3.    **Read or recite the Poem entitled "I See," page 114 often  to remind yourself of our
enemy's true intentions.**

4.    **Listening.**  We listen to become one with the Divinely quiet spirit inside of us that is
connected to the rhythm of this universe or higher vibration.  It is most attainable when you are
quiet and concentrating on your breathing.   Loud noise of any kind negatively impacts your
availability to listen and receive.   Spend a few minutes each day just listening.  Take note that
we have two ears and one mouth.  Listen twice as much as you talk.

5.    **Again, daily example and express gratitude**      First, learn to always be grateful no
matter how challenging life has or may become.  Show and embrace gratitude daily, *say I am
grateful beyond measure*. Thanks for things being as well as they are today.  Embrace a daily
"attitude of  gratitude (Christian Larson)" no matter the challenges life throws at you.

**6.** **Self-Forgiveness** It is critical to forgive yourself for past failures, hurts, and negative actions. We have all come short of being the best person in every circumstance in our lives. Self-forgiveness is necessary to begin the healing process. Say "I forgive myself for past wrongs, including thoughts, words, and deeds." Forgive yourself for you cannot un-ring the bell.

**7.** **Self-Realization** Occurs when you have grown to appreciate your greatness and begin developing your potential and living your purpose.

**8.** **Service** Acts of kindness and sincere outreach to help those in distress and support and take care of our elderly is inherit in our ancestral DNA. Acts of genuine service and kindness are extended without intended reciprocity.

**9.** **Study** Start with Gratitude and Assertions. Study is lifelong in our community. Adults who usually read parent children who love reading. Adults who make solid academic performance the centerpiece of their child's academic career and as a prerequisite for extra curricula participation, produce children who can compete in the Universal Economy. Read a cross section of information. Adults who always example putting forth your best effort, raise children who do the same.

> **Some Theorists maintain the mind is a well-oiled machine and must be fed throughout our lives. In-depth study across a myriad of subjects is an integral part of daily life**.

**Study: Read, Read, Read**

***Books of Faith*** **(you choose)**

***The Writings of*** **Fredrick Douglas**
   ***Alondra Drakes, Dick Gregory***

***Books and writings*** **by Dr. Henry Louis Gates, Jr.**

*The Writings of* **TD Jakes, Neil Degrasse Tyson,  Marcus Garvey, Dr. Cornell West, Toni Morrison, Ta-Nehisi Coates**

***The Power of Intention*** By Dr. Wayne W. Dyer
***The Seven Spiritual Laws of Success*** by Deepak Chopra

***The Autobiography of Malcolm*** **X** by Alex Haley

***Poetry*** **by Mya Angelou, Gwendolyn Brooks, Langston Hughes, and  lcookhamilton**

***Hidden Figures*** by Margaret Lee Shetterly, and many more.

**The Constitution of the United States of America**

**Your State Constitution and your local ordinances**

___________________________________________________

List your favorites here

___________________________________________________

___________________________________________________

___________________________________________________

**10.    <u>Strength Training</u>**    Extremely important and is necessary for toning, keeping the muscles supple, and releasing negative energy caught in the body.  It is critical for maintaining proper posture and good balance throughout your life.

**<u>Tai Chi</u>**    A very doable practice for the elderly that supports good balance and mental alertness.  It is a must for the elderly, yet it is a valuable exercise for any age.

**<u>Yoga</u>**    Is critical for muscle and bone health, stress relief, flexibility, overall relaxation, connectivity, and endurance.  It is believed to help with immunity. **Yoga and strength training** are critical to good health, a sound mind and enduring skeletal structure. **<u>Further Study</u>** will help us understand Cascadian Systems, Charkas, and connecting to our Third Eye.

**<u>Mediation</u>** Meditation stills and quiets the mind, enabling you to listen, focus, receive, and become aware of possibilities that compliment  and illuminate your purpose.  It helps rid your mind of greed, hatred, and delusion.  It helps you interact with your pure energy and the third eye.  Quietness and being still matters.  It helps to boost confidence and diminish stress levels and release you to immerse yourself in the present moment.  It is important to quiet the mind.  Chose a type of Mediation likable to you: Mindfulness, Prayer, Chant, Zazen, Deepak Chopra/Oprah, Tantra, Japa, Transcendental, or choose your preference.

Use a mat, cushion, small bench, or chair if necessary. When meditating, you may want to face the Motherland, Africa, out of appreciation and respect.   Practice the Meditation you   have chosen.

Or here is a simple meditation:  Lay down a mat or clean floor covering of your choice facing the Motherland.  Sit in the Lotus position with your  hands opened and resting on the top of your knees and facing upward.   Close your eyes.  Inhale deeply through your nose for five counts expanding your stomach muscles.  Exhale through your nose for seven counts contracting your stomach muscles.  Repeat eight times.   As tons of thoughts try to enter your mind, concentrate on the breath count bringing yourself back to center.

During Meditation, whenever your mind wonders, go back to breath counts to re-center yourself and bring you to the present.

Duration:  Thirty minutes or longer depending on the type.  If time is limited, try 8 minutes, and really focus.

**Overall, we must value a healthy mind and body, exercise daily,  read and study, and teach our children to do the same.  Children learn by our examples.**

# <u>*Mantra Entitled "I See"*</u>

*(by L.CookHamilton)*

I See, my Mind and Soul are free

And the internal trauma is put out to sea

I have healed the hole in my soul and now pride myself on being wholesome me.

**I am** the chosen, the gifted, the invincible that I now see

**And yet**, I will never forget Robert E. Lee

And his intended insidious condition for me.

I now trod in coalescence with my people

As we face the Motherland and speak

To the souls of the ancestors *to* not moan or weep.

For I will claim our destiny without haste

And secure our righteous place.

**M**y determination and fortitude run deep

Your sacrifices and endurances in my heart I keep

As the motivation to always be the best I can be

**Because I SEE, and now I am mentally free.**

*( Even recite this poem as **a  group, with hands to heart  at family or community gatherings** as the call to order.)*

# <u>Self-Empowering Module II</u>   Building Strong and Self-sustaining Families

## *Family Unit*

The smallest and most important structural unit in the A-A culture is "The Family," and it must be structurally and functionally healthy for our people, our culture, and our communities to be viable and economically self-sufficient.  Consider the man as the tree and the woman as the root. Men must be men in that the man must stand upright and support his family including respecting his wife and actively participate in raising his children to be productive citizens by modeling self-respect, quality character traits, academic achievement, and good citizenship.  Sidney Poitier said, "The measure of a man is how well he takes care of his family."  The man must be the Central Figure and Head of the Family and not the tail.  He must model for a boy how to be a viable father figure and supporting husband. The formation of children's values, their self-actualization, boundaries, and modes of behavior are the responsibility of their parents.

A solid harmonious, wholly, and productive family unit is critical to the sustainability of our people.  This is not difficult to see because in nature, it takes a man and a woman to make a child. It follows, that it requires both to raise the children.   In general, a woman cannot effectively teach a boy how to be a man.  Often, a woman will raise him to be weak, dependent, and most importantly ill equipped about how to be a man and how to treat and take care of his own wife and children as the central figure in the home and to be the iconic example to his children.

Our community must build on stable, secure, families with a father(tree) mother(root) and hopefully with three or more children. Self-sustaining, educationally focused, and civic minded Family Units are the Pillars of the A-A community.

## ***Educate our Children (Watoos) to become their best selves.***

Education, learning, and advanced training are another hallmark of a self-sustaining community. Parents are the first and the most important teacher and overall educator of their children, not schools.  Schools exist to assist parents in the education of their children. The first step in educating children is making them feel loved, safe, and secure.  Then teaching and demanding of them respect, modeling for them self-appreciation, hard work, self-respect, manners, dignified speech, and serious study habits across multiple subjects.   Always demand from them sincere efforts to master subject matter. Extra-curricular activities are an option <u>only after </u>mastery of subject matter.  Developing an erudite is our task as parents and as a community.

Together, lets educate our Watoos (children) in their neighborhood schools.  Our Watoos do not necessarily have to attend school with European American children to be great.  Take a lesson from the movie "Lean on Me," and stand tall, raising descent, law abiding, socially civil students in their neighborhood schools.  As taxpayers, demand proper funding for our schools by using the power of the Vote.  Advocate for ourselves and take responsibility for the education of our children ourselves.  We must do for ourselves.  Clean up our schools.  Volunteer, donate, and evaluate the quality of learning.  Most of all, parent respectful children who go to school to learn and apply themselves without nonsense, bullying, and lack of focus.  Establish quality study time at home year-round.  Study is an integral part of everyday life for both children and parents. If you demand the best from your Watoo, his/her best is what  you will get.

# Remove Toxins.

Purge negative, toxic people, toxic environments, and toxic situations from your life immediately. Again, let go of toxic people, places, and environments. These pollute and block your connection to positive energy, and at times even slowing it down enough to invite more negativity to seep into your daily life.  When your life condition is low, it attracts from the four lower universal life conditions: hell, anger, self-destruction, and apathy.  Remember the shadow follows the body.  Seek to be in rhythm with higher vibration.

> *"Change the way you look at things and the things you look at change."*
>
> Dr. Wayne Dyer

As you know, toxicity can be a cause of disease, anxiety, and substance abuse.  It opens your internal dialogue to destructive and unproductive suggestions.  Remove the toxins.

# Self-Actualization.

We self-actualize when you live  your purpose by fully developing your potential, talents, and rearing your children to do the same. This requires a serious attitude, concentrated study,  good character, and a commitment to live the underlying law of this Universe:  which is **Cause and Effect** also described in many writings as What ye Sow...

<u>**Self-Empowering Module III**</u>    **Civic Involvement:**

<u>**Vote in Every Election**</u>

<u>**Stay Abreast of the Issues Yourself**</u>

Exercise Your Civic Duties Relentlessly: Vote no matter what. Teach this to your children.  Take them with you when you vote or watch you fill out  the paperwork to vote by mail or enter the screen data to vote online.  Let them see that voting is critical in every election.  Make it an activity that **the Family** does together.

**V** = **Voice and value, how we as a people speak to power.**

**O** = **Omnipotent, we wield unlimited power when we vote
and thereby honor our Ancestors.**

**T** = **Truth, we see clearly.  Our eyes are fully opened.**

**E** = **Emancipated from Mental Slavery.**

By employing our votes and purchasing power, we will be relentless in pressuring the Congress and the Supreme Court to uphold the Constitution of the United States of America, the projected model of Democracy for the world to emulate.  No longer will injustice be tolerated against the A-A Community.  Our laser focus is on the just application of these Amendments: 1, IV, V, VI,13, 14, 15, 19, and 24, and Articles 1, II, III, IV and V.

What more can we do? First make sure you vote, then employ the 3by3 rule.  Find and take to the polls three people who would not vote unless you ensured their participation.   Remember to make sure they are registered and where they vote.  This is no small matter.  Do your part, always fulfill the **3by3 rule**.  Stop complaining and making excuses. Instead, become an active participant in the affairs of government.

Demand flexible opportunities to exercise your Constitutional Right to vote: Voting by mail, voting on weekends, voting in person, cyber voting, etc. Demand through whom you elect to office that the focus is on allowing as many registered voters as possible to vote.

Attend your local public meetings of the Councils, Commissions, Boards, etc. and meet often with your state and national elected representatives and *respectfully* voice what is right and just for our community.  Study your State Legislative Sessions. Prepare a representative caucus to visit law makers during session.  Use all forms of communication/ media to let them know what is just and right for our people.

| **John Lewis** |
| --- |
| U.S. Representative, Civil and Voting Rights Icon.  Served as Chairman of the Student Nonviolent Coordinating Committee (SNCC) 1963 to 1966. |
| "Ordinary people with extraordinary vision can redeem the soul of America by **getting in good trouble,** necessary trouble.  Vote and participate in the democratic process." |
| **Books:** Walking with the Wind: A Memoir, March:  Book One |

Always vote strategically for the betterment of our people and never allow yourself to be bamboozled.  Read and study the issues for yourself.  Do not depend on other.  You must know for yourself.

For an educated mind is rarely bamboozled with deceptive rhetoric and dog whistle politics.

**Read and commit to memory the Poem entitled  "Like Me" on page 50 of this book.**


<u>**Self-Empowering Module IV**</u>   **Maintain Neat and Clean Surroundings and Living Spaces**

***<u>Schedule Community Clean-up and Fix-up days.</u>***  Perhaps every 5th Saturday or Sunday.  We need a new determination and attitude which expounds our communities will be places of decency, integrity, cleanliness, and lawfulness. Never burn or loot where you live. During the Wicked Time, they forced us to live like animals in the hope that we would continue to do so as part of the residual effect.  **We see clearly now** and will live in pristine and lawful places because we will make them so.   Clean Up and fix up.   Remove debris, broken vehicles, and general blight to its designated places for which you pay taxes.  Do not litter, ever and we have back yards for a reason… Use them.  Every activity at your dwelling does not warrant an ostentatious display for the entire public to see.  Share less, please.

# <u>Self-Empowering Module V</u>  Develop and Support Economic Infrastructure

**<u>*Relentlessly practice Umoja (unity), Ujamaa (cooperative economics).*</u>**  We must practice unity in all things.  We must develop as entrepreneurs and build a solid economic infrastructure in our communities.  We need to own and support our businesses and services.  These businesses and services must be reliable, honest and deliver a quality product or service. We must have A-A economic leadership in our communities.  Our ancestors gave us the example of Black Wall Street in Tulsa Oklahoma that was maliciously, and wickedly destroyed by racial terrorists.  This was a very viable example of community sufficiency.  Next time however, we must be prepared and willing to *protect* what is ours - no matter what.

Booker T. Washington said, "*hard work, material prosperity, and cultivation of the **virtues of patience, enterprise, and thrift*** is important."

**The Gees Bend Quilters** of Wilcox Alabama whose skill has  passed from generation to generation.

**<u>*A few  Entrepreneurs over the years*</u>**: "Negro Wall Street in the Greenwood District of Tulsa," Stephen Smith, Annie Malone, Cathy Hughes, Frederick Patterson, North Carolina Mutual Life Insurance Company,  Maggie Walker  and the  St. Luke Penny Savings Bank, Madam C.J. Walker,  M. R. Beal & Co., Andrew Young,  James Forten, Earl Graves, Jr., Barry Gordy, John H. Johnson, Oprah Winfrey,  McKissick Construction,  Reginald F. Lewis, Bee Smith, Tyler Perry, Eugene R. Hudson,  Spike Lee and His Forty Acres,  A. G. Gaston  of Birmingham,  Michael Jordan,  Jay -Z, P Diddy,  Magic Johnson, Greg Calhoun of Montgomery, H. L. Wright & Company,  and many others

Your List :_________________________________

_________________________________

# Self-Empowering Module VI   Become Multi-lingual

To be competitive in the Universal Economy, we must speak at least two languages in addition to proper English. Consider, Chinese and Spanish, etc.  Make language study a part of the community and offer centralized language classes. Value study and learning until the end of this life and beyond.  Multi-lingual study is more easily grasped between the ages of two and eight. Our children will be well served to master the Spanish language by 2040 to maintain job marketability.

# Self-Empowering VII   Contribute Positively to our Culture and Community

1.   ***Practice Kujichagulia (self-determination)*** We define ourselves, create for ourselves, speak for ourselves, and name ourselves.  We do not skin and grin begging to be liked.  We do not laugh unless we deem something is truly funny, and we do not scratch unless we itch.

We live in *Appreciation of our Divine Beauty*. We must see our divine beauty and do  not measure it through the lens of European Americans.  We are grateful for our skin pigmentation and its abundance of melanin.  It will withstand the coming warming of the planet.

Embrace our Divinely given hair.  Our hair is a source of strength and a symbol of our glory, so protect it.  We care for it as a badge  of honor every day and feel blessed for its strength which will help protect us with the coming warming of the planet.  Of course, sometimes coloring is used to compliment skin pigmentation.  The color spectrum is not owned by anyone. As a matter of fact, the ancient Egyptians used color to highlight their eyebrows and facial features.  And Henna grows in tropical climates such as Africa.  It was used to dye hair and for body paint as far back as 3,400 BCE.  We are proud of our Divine hair and will seek to emulate no one.

2.      **Sunday Dinners with Family.**  This long-standing cultural ritual is to be embraced with the upmost of dedication, commitment, and appreciation.   Most respectfully at the home of the eldest person in the family residing in the area when available.  Sunday afternoons should be spent with family so younger generations and elders remain close and youth can be taught their vast history, learn respect for the elderly, and have proper manners reinforced.  ***All Organizations should respect this tradition and encourage families to go home by 1 P.M. and be together.*** This is a time to cook together and play together in peace, harmony, and love.  This peaceful and love extending event includes, playing sports, studying our history, reciting poems, readings, singing, dancing, and listening to the sages.  It is not a time for social improprieties or arguments.  Excessive mind-altering substances, cursing ,  and profane behaviors are forbidden at these events. Strong families build strong communities.

This time-honored ritual  is foundation laying for our culture.  Our ancestors established Sunday afternoons as the time for our families to come together in unity and harmony.  It was the only time they had a break from the fields of hard labor. Let us honor this invaluable tradition and use it to build healthy wholesome families.

Other cultures pride themselves on embracing and carrying out their traditions. Traditions are the glue that hold a community together.  We need to honor more of our traditions.

3.    ***Take personal accountability to contribute positively to our communities and culture.***  Each of us as individuals and collectively as a community are accountable to look at our actions across all mediums and spheres (parental, spiritual, entertainment, sports, communications, etc.) and identify how we have contributed to the rot that has engulfed our community in a cycle of self-destruction including killing our own brethren, and resulting in many youth having an attitude that reflects a lack of seriousness about education.  If any of us have written, spoken, shown, sang, performed, acted in a role, worked at, or did anything to have encouraged or nurtured the lack of respect and hate many of us act on towards each other, even insulting our mothers and sistahs; then you must immediately take personal responsibility for your contribution to this mental slavery.  You must spend just as much time and money reversing what has been done by teaching love and support for your fellow brother.  You taught them to die, now teach them to live productively and with honor and dignity. Cause and effect are absolute.  You cannot create sorrow in other families and not expect it to reverberate back into your family somewhere down the generations.

*Lonnie G. Brunch III,*

*Historian*

***Charlene Hunter Gault***

***Maulana Karenga***

**The Little Rock Nine**

***Leroy Graves****, Historic*

*Conservationist*

***Dr.  Christine Mann***

***Darden****, Aeronautical*

*Engineer*

***C.T. Vivian, Civil Rights***

*Leader*

No matter our circumstances or sufferings, we should muster the ichinin (determination) to share the truth in a caring way and not an angry, self-destructive way.  Bob Marley wrote and sang about many experiences and he never resorted to sharing negativity that would undermine our community or cause us to turn on each other in rage and disregard for life.

4.      ***Honor and teach our History*** at home, at school, at family dinners,  in religious houses, temples, mosques, centers of worship, cultural centers, family reunions, etc.   Here are a few suggestions: *Films* by Sankofa, Haile Gerima, Mangamizi, The Ancient One by Ron Mulvihill, 500 Years Later by Owens Shahadah, and When the Spirits Danced the Mambo by Marta Mereno Vega. *Consult historical  writings* by Dr. Henry Louis Gates, Jr., Dr. Cornell West, John Hope Franklin, Nelson Mandela, Georges Nzongola-Ntalaja, Dr. Maulana Karenga, Frederick Douglas, PBS,  visit the National Museum of A-A History & Culture, and others.

*Read, read, read*

Arika L. Coleman
   ***"That Blood Stay Pure"***
Edward E. Baptist
   ***"The Half has Never Been Told"***
Lerone Bennett, Jr.
   ***"Before the Mayflower"***

***The Constitution of the Unites States of America***

*Alex Haley* ***"Roots"***
***Jacqueline Woodson***
***Add yours*** _______________
_______________________

5.      ***Practice the Festival of Lights*** (*the first Saturday Night in October*).   A festival to celebrate the victory of good over evil in our daily lives and our communities overall,  the attraction of good health and prosperity throughout the community or tribe, in honor of new babies having arrived, and in gratitude for a great harvest.   See the sequel to this book for specifics on the Festival of Lights Ceremony.

6.    ***Practice Kwanzaa*** *from December 26th to January 1st annually to culminate in a Grand Family and or  Community Celebration on December 31st.*   Consult Dr. Karenga who has written extensively about Kwanzaa. See the sequel to this book for specifics on the culminating ceremony.

7.    ***Ragtime*** *and* ***Jazz****: embrace and behold this genre of music created by us over several hundred years, much of that time, without our being able to read or write.* **Jazz is born out  Ragtime and encompasses  the generations of struggle by our ancestors and associated experiences in America.**  Although we were not allowed to read, we could play and sing beautifully.  It encouraged  togetherness, peace, and harmony within our communities. *Can you Scat, play the many instruments, and just jam for the pure enjoyment and spirituality of it all*? What about the concentration and phrasing? Jazz, the freedom to create on the fly and let your mind wonder precipitously.   We must learn to play the instruments, sing, and dance to the rhythms.  Try Bebop.  Scat, croon, and holler. **Listen to Jazz so the young will know and embrace their history.**   Don't you agree that every child  should learn to play at least one instrument?

*Learn about some of the elders of Jazz and those who have sustained its existence*:  Miles Davis, Art Blakely, Duke Ellington, Lena Horne, Eubie Blake, Ella Fitzgerald, Dixieland, Sarah Vaughn, Billy Holiday, John Coltrane, The Marsalis's featuring Winton, Count Bassie, Charlie Parker, Norah Jones, Jasmeria Horn,  Dee Dee Bridgewater, Duke Ellington, Cecile Salvant, Shirley Horn, Emma  "Ginger" Smock, Reginald Veal, Louie Armstrong, Nat King Cole, Abby Lincoln, Diana Reeves, Dizzie Gillespie,  Billie Holiday, Dakota Station, Nina Simone, Billie Eckstein, Thad Jones, Clark Terry, Harry Edison, India Cook, Ray Charles, Max Roach, Sidney Bechet, Kid Ory, Joe Williams, Cassandra Wilson, Peggy Lee, Wycliff

Gordon, Todd Williams, Al Jerreau, Gregory Porter, Mose Allison, W. C. Handy, Jelly Roll Morton, Sonny Stitt, Joe Henderson, Lockjaw Davis, Reginald Veal,  Ornette Coleman, Sweet Emma Barrett, Matthew Whitaker, and Dr. Don Shirley, etc.   *Jazz is synonymous with our people.  We should pay homage to our very own **Jazz**.*

**Other genres where our people have excelled:**

***Rock n Roll*** whose father is Chuck Berry and  the Mother of Rock n Roll was  Sister Rosetta Tharpe.

***Rhythm and Blues*** **which led to Country**

***Rap and  Hip Hop***

**Gospel**


**Add your favorite musical influences here**: _________________________________,

_______________________________, _________________________________,

___________________________


Remember music and rhythm was part of our ancestor's cadences for millions of years in Africa before the African Holocaust, especially playing instruments such as the drums, kora, akoting, gourd (banjar that became the banjo), marimbula, mbira, balafon; singing and dancing.  Then, throughout our 400  years of human bondage here in the  Americas, we retained our natural connection to music especially playing instruments such as the drums, piano, woodwind instruments, guitar, banjo, and after 1865, writing, and producing.

8.       ***Dance often***.  Dancing and rhythm are a major part of our culture that we retained from Africa. It allows us to communicate without words. Dancing is healthy for the heart, body, and mind.  Dance the, juba, Charlestown, wop, twist, jitterbug, rumba, lindy hop, salsa, tango, two-step, running man, soul train line, tap, and line dances of all kinds, etc. Even dance on formal occasions, and why not try the Waltz and the Charleston. Remember to dance throughout your life for your health.  We should dance anytime, but even more when there is a full moon and on special occasions.  Examine the styles of Norma Miller, Marx Brothers, Lindy Hoppers, Free Styles, Alvin Ailey, Judith Jamison, Savion Glover, Charleston, The Dance Theatre of Harlem, Valada Snow, The Nicholas Brothers, Hines Brothers, Bill Robinson, and more recently the Subway Dancers, Hip-hop Dancers,  and Line dances of all types.   We stand in awe of Ballerina Misty Danielle Copeland.

9 .      ***Examine Self: Are you the rot***? *Know this*:  if a membership in anything or  the excuse of making money leads you to perpetuate circumstances or actions that harms your own people and community, creates turmoil and devaluing of life among your own people, then you are doing someone else's bidding who is hell bent on marginalizing or destroying our people.  You are the rot.  Check yourself.

Recite the poem entitled **"I See"** on page 113 of this book.

10.  ***Nyabinghis Gatherings ( named after an African Queen)***


**Define**: These are *Emergent Businesses Opportunity Seminars to be held in Community Centers, Halls, Family Rooms, Back Yards, etc.*
**Intention:** *To learn to become fierce competitors in the Universe Wide Business Sector.* ***To build and support our own economic infrastructure in our communities,***

## A Nyabingis Gathering

### Sample Agenda Items

**Open by listening to a little Jazz  and All recite the Poem  "I See," page 109.**

Next, always establish an **intention** for the Gathering, then meditate or pray for the intention to be realized.

**Begin with item I or rearrange the order to suit your needs.**

I.  A What's Coming Segment:  Emerging Global Trends, Influencers,  and projected Business Models on the horizon.

II.  Study Universal Business Status and Opportunities

Attendees study from Black Enterprise

Study a broad spectrum of solid economic

information:

The Bureau of Economic Analysis

Franchising Opportunities

US Federal Reserve

The Council of Economic Advisors


Bloomberg and the Wall Street Journal
Index

The African Development Bank
Inter-American Development Bank
International Financial Statistics
Asian Development Bank

III.    Review Finance: recent Stock, Bond, Futures, and Commodities, Currencies including Crypto, etc., and    International Trading Activities and Markets

IV.    Review Recent Reports from the Better Business Bureau

V.    Review Recent Reports from the Bureau of Labor Statistics, the U.S. Treasury, and your local Chamber of Commerce

VI.    Review Recently Released  Information from the U.S. Census Bureau.  Pay close attention to your State and Local census numbers

VII.    Review Recently Released Information from the IRS

VIII.    Study New and Emerging Technologies on the Global Horizon including medical, cyber, social, crypto, transport, virtual, artificial intelligence, telecommunications, information  technologies, planetary travel,   environmental, oceanic, follow what is transpiring in gene modification or so-called designer babies, robotics, etc.  Add new technologies to the list as they emerge.  Stay abreast of emerging technologies.

IX.    Review data from the Department of Homeland Security, the Food and Drug Administration,  the Department of Health and Human Services, the Center for Disease Control, The Federal Communications Commission,  the Department of Environmental Protection, and the Securities and Exchange Commission.

X.    Review recent updates and status reports from The  U.S. Department of Education, your State Department of Education, and your Local School Board

XI.    Review recent updates from the Department of Veterans Affairs

XII.    Review legislation being discussed at the state, national, international, and universal levels.

You may choose to focus on  several of these topics at a Nyabangis Gathering  or **all** if you are so inclined.  There is no specific order of the agenda.  You may want to start with the Department of Education.

***At the end of the session:  Stand and recite the poem "I SEE" on page 114 of this book as if your life depended on it.***

11.    ___Support each other___.  ***If you cannot support a brother or sistah trying to do something positive, shut the hell up.  Do no harm.*** **Why is it so easy** to find one of us that will criticize the other outside of our community or tribe especially in the media, online, or to others outside of our community?  No one respects a sell-out, not even the people you are selling out to.  You see, they know that if you go against your own people, you have no character and cannot be trusted.  Notice how conveniently one of us is usually made front and center to  lead a charge against or to confront one of our own.

12.    **Tattle none.**   Crab Mentality None.  Do no harm.  Close your mouth and stop pulling down your own people.  If you are always speaking negatively about others, then negativity will surely find you, because misery and negativity is what you are seeking.  The same is true of a people or community.  Stop running and tattling, skinning, and grinning.

13.    **Defend Our Own.**  Hear us clearly now, we will defend our families, our communities, and our vote with our lives.  Hear us now!!! NEVER AGAIN will we be denied our human and voting rights.  Bob Marley ask, "How long shall they kill our prophets (men and boys) while we stand aside and look"?   What happen to Black Wall Street for example, will not happen again, and go unanswered…

14.   **<u>Commit to learning.</u>**  Reading and studying are a life-long endeavor.

15.   Fasting.  Remember to participate in fasting.  Fasting provides clarity of mind, increases energy, and allows the brain and overall body to convalesce.

16.   Determine to live your life such that after you exit, your community is left better than you found it at birth. We owe it to our ancestors to engage in serious work and reject frivolous nonsense especially engaging in over the top loudmouth speech, lazy grammar, half nude attire, braggadocios language, demeaning of self and others, poor parenting, poor participation in the education process, and for some promiscuity.  *Each of us* is accountable to model for our youth: decency, modesty, respectfulness,  good character, and how to utilize fortunate life blessings to live their purpose, be respectful, family centered, a productive benefit to their community, and to become life-long learners.

> Muhammad Ali said "**Don't count today, make today count.**
>
> **<u>Service</u> to others is the rent you pay for your room here on  earth.**"

17.   We demand true accounting and factual inclusion in the United States History books. No longer will our profound history be relegated to a few lines, or a picture with a few lines of commentary.  We demand a true and factual writing of United States History. Better yet, we will write it ourselves.  A certain State's version of U.S. history that appears in the History Books is disingenuous to be kind, while controlled by one large state in the South with its Juneteenth history.

<u>Self-Empowering *Module VIII*</u>      *Youth Ceremonies*

## Rites of Passage

1.  **A-A Male Rite of Passage to Manhood "A-A Male Rite ."**

    Preparation begins at age 12 and culminates at age 14.   It lays the foundation  or platform for development into a self-sustainable family supporting man.

2.  ***A*-A Young Female "Melanin Cotillion."** Preparation begins at age 13 and

    culminates at age 15.

3.  **Watoo  (Child) Introduction**

    ***A*-A Watoo Gathering.**  The introduction of a newborn is made to the community

    after three full moons.   Referred to as **The Watoo Gathering**.  Invitees come

    bearing gifts, prayers and blessings.

<u>Thank you</u> **for choosing to empower yourself.   It is true that a change in one's fundamental mindset can lead to *a change in one's life, immediate environment, and ultimately the entire world.*  It is time for meaningful change at the grass roots level of our communities with the targeted intention of self-sustainability for our individual families and by extension our culture**.

*Recite the poem  "I See" on page 113 of this book*

# Chapter 9

## Message to Parents

Parents have an obligation to set an example of how to live, to serve, and to be self-sustaining based on hard work, serious academic study, and your faith of choice. Parents teach children to respect boundaries and most of all how to respect self. Fulfilling parental responsibilities are essential to the emotional well-being of the child, his/her cognitive development, positive self-esteem, and academic commitment and civic awareness. When the parent's eyes are opened, the Watoto (child in Swahili) grows up secure and confident in who they are and embrace their vast potential which is second to none in the Universe.  Remember, children to not become what we as parents teach, they tend to become who we are as a person. For example, a violent father often rears a violent son and a daughter who subjects herself to violence from a mate.

On the contrary, a child who grows up in a home where parents read, study, meditate and or pray, play instruments, exercise, eat healthy, is law-abiding and civic participating; will gravitate towards the same basic life tendencies as adults. Parents  must engage in sound cognitive and emotional development encapsulated in  empathy, positive self-worth, a commitment to self-sustainability, and service.  Seek to nurture mental and physical prowess that are innate to our being and bring forth the character traits established eons ago in the Motherland Africa:  invincibility, grit, fortitude, resourcefulness, family stability, community protection, and the 5Ss. *These are the hallmarks of good parenting.*

*Know that Watotos must dedicate their formative years to laying the foundation for self-actualization (living their purpose).  Achieving self-actualization is necessary to ensure happiness and fulfillment as an adult.  Parents must focus on removing barriers to a Watoto being able to create the foundation that will lead to self-actualization.*

The solid self-sustaining family unit (fathers, mothers, children, grandparents, aunts, uncles, etc.)  is the most critical component to our survival as a people and as a culture.

Your children need nurturing, secure, trusting, and healthy relationships with their parents and extended family as these are critical to forming a solid foundation for quality social and emotional development, and self-actualization.   Children need secure and trusting relationships with their parents.   Keep your children away from adverse childhood experiences that will lead to barriers to learning, emotional scars, a lack of self-worth, out of control anger,  and a lack of seriousness towards academics.  Parents demand your children perform at his/her highest academic level.

The formation of children's values and modes of behavior is the responsibility of the parents.  Children learn to think, speak correctly,  reason, and respect when they are young. They learn responsibility and consequences of their actions with parental assistance and never forget that boundaries help children stay in their righteous place and space.

*Instead of keeping skin color foremost in our children's minds*, we should teach them their culture, traditions, their invincibility, mental and physical prowess.  Cultures remain strong because they cling to and maintain their wholesome traditions and solid family structure.  Developing and maintaining solid, wholesome families are the bedrock of our continued universal existence.

### *Little Eyes Upon You*

Author unknown

There are little eyes upon you
And they are watching night and day.
There are little ears that quickly
Take in every word you say.
There are little hands all eager
To do anything you do.
And a little boy who is dreaming
At the day he will be like you.

You are the little fellow's idol,
You are the wisest of the wise.
In his little mind about you
No suspicions ever rise.
He believes in you devoutly,
Holds all that you say and do.
He will say and do, in your way,
When he is grown up like you.

There is a wide-eyed little fellow
Who believes you're always right.
And his eyes are always opened,
And he watches day and night.
You are setting an example
Every day in all you do,
For the little boy who is watching
To grow up to be like you.

# I am a Gift on Loan

by L.CookHamilton

As I circled the cosmos waiting to be assigned to you
Through the intersection of sperm and egg is how I usually get through
I wondered what you, my parents, would do.
Will you understand that I am a gift on loan and not something for you to own.

Will you teach me to be responsible, kind, and true?
And a compliment to my people in the things I do!!
You were blessedly chosen to be a parent, a noble charge indeed
Will you fare and stand tall, entrusted with the Divine's greatest gift of all
Or drop like a dead autumn leaf in the Fall.

I am a gift on loan and under your control
What a mighty responsibility to behold.
Is instilling the values of hard work, good character, discipline, and
lifelong pedagogy your goals?

It is your examples that I will value and extend to my children with glee
For they will carry on your legacy you see
Embracing those same character traits, you gave me
To extend down the generations as a tribute to thee.

I am just a gift on loan, I dare say
So, teach me the right way.
Earth is but a temporary home
And remember one day we will both be gone
Back into the cosmos having made the world better or worst.

A-A men are authentic with great mental and physical prowess, honorable, trustworthy, and great financial supporters and providers for their wives and children.  You are the head of the household and not the tail.  The leader and the Protector.  A real man.  A-A men are gentlemen: your word is your bond, you keep your promises, you are respectful, kind, and pull your wife's chair in a restaurant.   A-A men know these things:

> **A-A men must stand strong at the head of the household. I was once told by a Rabbi: "if the man is weak; the overall culture will never be strong."** Heed these words.

1. Your successful role underscores the security and stability of the family.  You are the tree of the family.  The family has a tremendously difficult task standing tall if the tree is weak, bending and breaking even when the weather is fair.

2. Many outside our community engage in ruthless tactics to keep the male weak, self-hating, incarcerated; and subjected to a troll police state regardless of many being decent hardworking people.  This ensures the culture can never be strong.  While this effort is alive and well, but we must outsmart it by embracing the 5s.

3. Every conceivable effort is made to marginalize you, in fact, destroy you or act as the puppeteer to watch you wantonly destroy yourself and your fellow brethren. Be

> *"Don't  let a set-back be a stay-back"*
> *Kenya  J. Hamilton*

aware of the pitfalls used to animus A-A men.  For high A-A financial achievers, the accusation will almost always involve private body parts, alleged out of control anger, or character assassination of some kind.   For other A-A men there is an assumption of weapons carry, simply walking while A-A, or even being in your own home or back yard, not to mention walking down the street while A-A.   We must get ourselves together and take control of our communities, so we will no longer be killed, framed, shown indifference, or destroyed in the public sphere based on the flimsiest evidence or outright untruths.   It is critical that we demand that those who patrol our communities, live there, pay taxes there, shop there, send their kids to school there.

4. Be aware. The favorite tool used to undermine, discredit, and often destroy the successful African American male, whether a teacher, athlete, entertainer, sports commentator, minister, etc. will, nine times out of ten, have to do with his private body part or anger in some fashion or another. The A-A is wholly discredited and loses everything on the weakest of evidence while the EA Male will continue to make millions, still respected, and even elevated.

5. The same accusations involving an A-A male will never die because they will be rehashed and rehashed

6. Yes, A-A men are subjected to gross injustice.   But the grossest injustice is what they do to each other.

7. Do not dawdle.  Do not procrastinate. Teach this to your children.

   Read about the Black Panther Party for Self-Defense.  The Black Panther Party was about self-help, feeding the hungry in the community, providing health care, voting in every

> **A glaring example of destruction through law enforcement framing and targeting for destruction is the Black Panther Party for Self-Defense.**
>
> **Some Members of the Black Panther Party were:**
>
> Huey Newton
>
> Bobby Seale
>
> Stokley Carmichael
>
> H. Rap Brown
>
> Kathleen Cleaver
>
> Tarika Lewis
>
> Assanta Shakur
>
> Erica Huggins
>
> Dr. Rose Mari Mealy
>
> **They** were about good work in  our communities

election, fighting for justice at every turn, and standing up to protect their families and community.

8. As courageous descendants from ancestors who survived the Wicked Time, we know that a sword in the hands of a coward is useless.  When necessary, you may be required to be father and mother.  Stand tall and always take care of your children.  Your children are your priority.

9.  Boys develop their character traits from their fathers.  If father is present in his live and is kind, loving, financially supportive, and protective; the son will value these traits into manhood.  Now imagine the void if the father is deliberately missing from the boy's life.  Something or someone must fill the void.  Often destructive tendencies arise, and unhealthy group alignments are chosen to fill the void.

So, fathers are fundamental to how a boy feels about himself and the character he carries into manhood.  Fathers show girls how to be treated by a man: care, love, support, and respect.  I often wonder, how could a man walk around on this earth every day and not know if his child is hungry, safe, warm in winter, in a loving

---

**44<sup>th</sup> President of the United States**

**Barack Hussein Obama II,** is a true example of an authentic,  honorable, accomplished A-A man, husband, father, Community Organizer, Constitutional Scholar, and Senator.  He is academically accomplished, a great financial provider to his family, a man who lives the example of hard work, self-respect, grace, dignity,  good character, confidence, and remains undaunted by the hurling of every undermining evil at him.  He stood and stands with grit as a man with respect for his manhood, the U. S. Constitution, his civil rights, and a solid supporter of his wife and children, and holds respect for *all communities*, and the world.  Take a page out of his playbook.

and nurturing environment... Or just simply not care?  We applaud the many grandfathers, uncles, coaches, and others who step in and "positively" fill the void left by the deliberately absentee fathers.   You are a blessing beyond measure.

***Thank you to those fathers who are standing up and being solid fathers to their children.***

10.      A-A men are trolled with disdain for three reasons: **your mental and physical prowess, your courage, and your melanin.**  Some in the power structure are ghastly afraid of how overpowering you would become if you simply developed to your potential and lived your Divine purpose.  The goal is to keep you off sure footing, so you will not realize your Divine greatness.

   **Model for your children how to bend in a strong wind and not break.**

11.  Throughout A-A history, if a group or organization, emerges that has at its core encouraging A-A men to be clean living, self-sustaining men who do not kowtow, skin and grin; it will be maligned, labeled as radical, and as mental slavery would have it, some in our own community will openly participate in ostracizing and defaming.  This is done to ignite our crab mentality and prevent us from respecting genuine success and strong manhood standing on self-worth and self-sustainability.

12.  A-A men always base your actions on the underlying premise that, unlike EA,  you are never forgiven for a mistake no matter the circumstances, or how sincerely you take steps to show rehabilitation.  You are simply replaced no matter how

**William H. Carney,** First A-A to win the Congressional Medal of Honor.
**Andrew Young**

**Percy Lavon Julian**

Sidney Poitier
***"Your dreams are as valid as you are prepared to make them"***

***James Bubba Stewart, Jr.,*** *Motocross Supercross Champion*

exceptionally skilled and valuable you thought you were to the group or team.  If you are A-A, your life mistakes will not be forgiven.   And if mistakes cannot be found legally, often some will be trumped up.  So be careful who you surround yourself with.  The Devil may be in your very orbit looking in your face daily.  Always remain alert, keep your eyes opened to what is transpiring and govern yourself accordingly.

**13.**　　**Men do not physically or mentally abuse women and children, ever.  You are the caretaker, their protector, their hero.   You example for your son how to value and treat a female, and you exampled for your female child how she should expect to be treated by a man.  The early values program young men and women to have a certain outlook or expectation in relationships.**

14.　　Finally, A-A men you are Whole and Complete.  You must realize and accept it.  You are unlimited with immense mental and physical prowess.  Use your anger and disappointments as fuel to propel you forward to living your best self, living your dreams, supporting your family and community, while fulfilling your Civic duties and making study as much a part of your daily life as breathing.  We must educate ourselves by reading, viewing, and listening to a cross-section of materials and information. For it is true that only viewing one side of a coin does not make one wise in the acknowledge of coins.

**Recite the poem "I See" on page 113 of this book.**

# As An A-A Man, I Stand

By L.CookHamilton

Now wait and let me tell you

You need to leave me be

For I am standing tall just like the strongest tree

Taking care of my wife and teaching my kids to study and to be all they can be

Loving my community and protecting it with pride and dignity.

So, take another look and see this real man

Taking care of his family by his very hands.

Teaching them our history and our roots including about faraway lands.

But if you want to know where you stand

I see you and your wicked hand

But you will not win because the face in the mirror is a REAL man.

No confusion here , **watch me as**

**I Stand,  I Stand!  Because I am a Man**

Women of A-A descent are cultured, graceful, physically fit, dependable, warm with a gentle touch, mentally astute, and courageous. A-A women strive to be graceful and charming; never loud, rude, undignified, and ostentatious.  She is like the roots of a tree, all over the place nurturing, teaching, being a mate, helping to support the family but never attempting to take the man's place in the home.

As woman, please be reminded of these things:
1. The man is the tree and the woman is the root.

    Mothers are multi-taskers who juggle  many things. Mothers nurture and train the children.  Children do not become how we raise them, they become who we are.  Do as I say and not as I do does not work.  Children see through to our true-life condition.

2. Push your husbands from the back.  Stop being confrontational and in his face.  Men hate this behavior and they tend to gravitate to women without these character traits.   Such in your face interactions with your husband, encourages the girl child to grow up to be a controlling, mouthy, confrontational female who struggles to attract or keep a descent husband.

3.  Another reason to stop taking control in the home where a providing father is present, is  when you do, it undermines the boy child's respect for his father and prevents the boy from growing into a strong supporting man.

4. Boys model themselves after their fathers especially character traits.  If father is loving, kind, supportive, self-reliant, and protective, the boy will adopt these traits.  In the

| |
| --- |
| **Harriet Tubman** |
| **Dr. Olivia Hooker** |
| **Miriam Makeba** |
| **Michelle Obama** |
| **Alicia Keys** |
| **Stagecoach Mary Fields of the U.S. Postal Service** |
| **Autherine Lucy** |
| **Fannie Lou Hamer** |

absence of a father figure, be careful the boy does not adopt unhealthy character traits or become overly reliant you.  A boy needs a genuine man to example for him how to respect and take care of women and girls.

5.  Teach academic discipline to your children.  Insist they focus on study as an investment in their future success and as the foundation necessary for adult self-sustainability.  Raise an erudite and never accept less than their best.

6.  As examples to our daughters, perhaps we should dress with a modicum of decency and self-respect as our A-A ancestors would appreciate.   Choosing hem lines on or below the knee and never exposing our private parts.  Decency, dignity, and self-respect.

7.  Many in the marketplace intentionally show us as loud, profane, verbally abusive, and often highly promiscuous even in roles as educated professionals.  Backstabbing, backbiting, lack of boundaries, loud, rude, unscrupulous, and projecting the worst.  Has our sense of decency and moderation passed down from our ancestors dissipated?  Perhaps it is time to examine how we are portrayed in the entertainment sector to <u>our sons and daughters</u>, not to mention the unfavorable

| |
| --- |
| **Phyllis Wheatley** |
| **Queens of Kush** |
| **Yasantawg** |
| **Princess Yennega** |
| **Mae Jemison** |
| **Winnie Mandela** |
| **Ruth Odom Bonner** |

impression we project to the world.  Do not sell our culture out for a few dollars.   Think about our youth.  **<u>Open your eyes.</u>**  Why deliberately portray immoral character traits that slant how our own children and  people of the world view us?  Unflattering and demeaning character traits teaches the world negative ideals about our culture and thus our children.  Of course, some like Cicely Tyson always embraces  her craft with decency and choses traits that serve as good examples to our children .

Now that we know better, do better.

8.  Women, we tend to raise our daughters and love our sons to weakness, many sons ending up unable or unwilling to thrive as a self-sustaining adult, still hanging around leeching off mom and sister.  This condition is of our own making.  Boys need a real man to example for him how to be a hard-working supporting provider with character, integrity, valuing education and a commitment to Civic duties.   Surrounding your son with a weak man who does not provide for the family, is a sure recipe for disaster for the male and female children. How can he learn how to be a man without positive self-sustaining male influence? *Stop coddling the boy child.*

9.  Perhaps we should seriously discuss the question "Is the taxpayer responsible to support someone because they engaged in sexual relations?"  Are the male and female participants responsible to provide?  It seems that if you cannot support a family, be careful not to have one.   For some, there is often a repeating cycle: get pregnant, get on the dole: WIC, TANIF, SNAP, welfare, etc.,  then live on the Dole for a lifetime and thereby teach dependency to another generation.  Generational government handouts in this country come with subliminal degrading messages.  As stated before, Governmental Assistance should be used to temporarily bridge a hardship gap such as losing your job or a death that removes financial support.   And there is no shame in seeking temporary assistance, however, it is a short-term remedy, and not a way of life and certainly not to be passed from generation to generation.

> **Ellen Johnson Sirleaf**
> *Former President of Liberia and the 1st Woman to win 5 million Ibrahim Prize for African Leadership*
>
> **Susan Rice, U.S. Ambassador**

Ask yourself, would the government be so generous with Welfare and Food Stamps unless there was a way to subliminally set you up to destroy you and your descendants.

There is no such thing as a free lunch, look around you.  It is very destructive to example this behavior to our girls and boys.  It pushes many of them towards a life of regret and exposes more children to adverse experiences and circumstances often fueling a diminished focus on serious academics, unnecessary barriers to learning, and thus failing at the necessary preparations to achieve self-reliance as an adult.

Dick Gregory

"Coconut milk is the only thing on this planet that comes identically to mother's milk"

10. The building of a nation (or community) starts with the woman because the mother is the first teacher of the child in the womb and the messages, she gives that child, the child gives the world.   Malcolm X.

11. Skin color is within our Mitochondrial DNA and is passed down from the mother. Dark pigment is believed to help protect us from the intensity of the sun's UV rays.

12. Women, our daughters and other girls are watching.  Live with respect for self, and value your self-worth by your actions not rhetoric. Mothers, work with Dad to raise adroit teenagers who will live with honor, integrity, and contribute positively to their community.

Mamie Elizabeth Till-Mobley

Maya Angelou

Valerie Jarrett

Claudette Colvin

Rosa Parks

Harriett Tubman

Oprah Winfrey

13. Again, mothers stop making excuses for your sons less they grow up to be weak men.  Only a strong man can model and teach a boy how to be a man.  Your overbearing simply makes the

 boy dependent and unproductive who then looks for a mother figure in a wife.  Never

allow an unproductive man around your

children.  It is against nature.

14. Music lessons including instruments and

vocals are important to childhood development.

15.  Women, we must resist the compelling urge

to openly dominate everything, although we are

the great multi-taskers of the Universe.  This is

very destructive inside the family and the

community at large.

16.  As women, lets agree today to generate positive energy and goodwill with class and

self-respect.

17.  As women, we must make every deliberate effort to feed our families wholesome  and

nutritious foods.  Recognizing that excessive

sugars, salts, processed meats, and sugary drinks

cannot replace fresh or frozen vegetables.   If you

focus on quality nutrition when they are young, it

will become a part of their everyday lives.

Our task is monumental and for generations, we have carried a heavy load uphill.  There is

none stronger in all ways as we A-A women.  Let  us refocus with clarity of mind and from

every corner of this country, get back to  raising our children to be global competitors in

science, technology, engineering, math, and the arts.

**Mother: To My A-A Male Child**

# Let Go

By LCookHamilton

I will be careful not to always step in front of you
I will relinquish and let you do
Hold your own bootstraps and construct your path too.

You will become a strong man who will never whence
For your grit, mental and physical prowess, fortitude, and invincibility, is
Divinely sent.

So, learn everything you can
Value your self-worth
Listen to the wisdom of the elders
As you navigate this harsh terrain

On your way to becoming a productive, family-supporting,
dignified, and self-sustaining man.

I am honored to be your mother, and let you stand.

Youth of A-A descent are sagacious, unafraid, mentally astute, with innate physical prowess, and a capable group.  Ancestors extended you endless fortitude, invincibility, and courage and the wisdom to know that you cultivate your inner strength from compassion for your fellow brethren and not from hostile actions towards them.  Recognize that hostile actions against your fellow brethren derive from mental slavery.

The years of your youth are foundation laying on which you will stand for the rest of your life.  If you neglect to apply yourself to serious preparation through discipline and study, you cannot un-ring a bell or live productively looking through the "wooda, shuda, kuda," rear view mirror (would have, should have, could have).

> **Neil DeGrasse Tyson**
> **John Legend**
> **Labron James**
> **Jackie Robinson  #42**
> **Frederick Douglas**
> **Will Smith**
> **Spike Lee**
> **Kobe Bryant  #24**
> **Denzel Washington**
> **Chadwick Bozeman**
>
> **44th President, Barack Obama**
>
> ***Read about:***
> Afrofuturism

During the 1960's and over the last few years, some A-A youth groups have courageously tried to expose the truth about the systemic lack of equal justice, and the failure of the United States to willingly extend basic rights supposedly guaranteed in the Constitution.  We hear you and applaud your efforts.

*M ale A-A Youth : Know these things:*

1.      Youth is the time of preparation, foundation laying, character, and emotional development.  Most of all it is the time of listening, learning from your parents and elders and focusing on academic opportunities.  Faith and religion are taught by your parents.

2.      Be receptive to listening and learning. Youth is the time when the foundations of life are modeled and taught to you.  Often referred to as the five Ss: Self-reliance, self-respect, self-determination, self-motivation, and self-sustainability.

3.      Be eager to study hard, exercise daily including yoga and strength training.  Eat sparingly (eat to live and not live to eat), low sodium and low sugar.  You may want to try Mediation or Mindfulness.  These practices put your life in harmony with the rhythm of this universe.

> **Emperor Menelik II** of Ethopia:
>
> Defeated Italy at the **Battle of Adwa in 1896** and retained the independence of his Country, <u>Ethiopia,</u> *against all odds and shocked the Imperialists.*
>
> **Ptahhotep 2400 B.C.**
>
> **The Papyrus 1600 B.C.**

4.      We improve ourselves as human beings when we encounter hardships.  Remember your mental and physical prowess is great beyond measure.  This has been proven time and time again beyond any doubt.  But you must devote your youth to harnessing  your tremendous gifts on your way to becoming a real man who is self-sustaining and supports his family.

5.      Today, in many ways the circumstances of your lives make you ever increasingly resentful, angry, and uncaring. I get it. The last four or five generations, you have been disappointed at the failure of the highly touted promises and expectations of your great

grand and grandparents for equality and equal justice in these United States as part of the Civil, Voting Rights Movements, and myriad of Court challenges.  While there have been some forward movement, respect for the basic human dignity of the A-A people, equal rights, and justice under the law continues to be in a dismal condition.  Most of you live under occupation in your own communities.

I get why you are angry and disappointed.  I question however, if you realize who you are punishing with the way you are lashing out.  **You are lashing out at your own people** who are just as victimized as you are and, in case of many elderly A-As, have endured oppression for an entire lifetime.  You are killing your own brothers and destroying families.  Check yourself.  Be careful not to become  the impetus or perpetuator of that which you say is unjust, cruel, and disrespectful of A-A lives.

6.     Equal rights are rarely given; they must be taken. In our case, a good place to start is in the classroom and in the voting booth.  **Frederick Douglas said, power concedes nothing without demand.  It never has and it never will.**

7.     Young A-As,  we from that in some years  as many as 10,000 young A-A boys and young men are killed annually by guns at the hands of their own brethren.  Most are

**Black Panthers  Party for Self-Defense  ( they modeled: stand  up and protect our own communities)**

**Scottsboro Boys**

**Stono Rebellion of 1739 led by Jeremy Cato**

**Million Man March of 2005 led by The Nation of Islam**

*Tommie  Smith  and  John Carlos 1968 Olympics.  After winning  gold  medals,  they raised their arms in salute to their ancestry.*

**Colin Kupernack and Eric Reid took a knee to protest racial injustice.  They made "good trouble"**

**Calvin Peate, Paul Robeson, Charles Luther Sifford**

**The Negro League**

purchased illegally.  Now let us examine the true impact of this evil action within our own communities.  Let us use an average of 3 children per male had he lived to reach 70.  Extrapolate.  3x10,000=30,000 votes lost per election.  70-18=52 years of being able to vote.  Assume one election every two years or 26 occurrences x 30,000 votes is 780,000 votes that could have been cast.  Just think about how many elections across the country could have gone in our favor if we were not doing the bidding of the enemy

Show me your friends and I will show you your character. Bad friends will keep you from having good friends.

and killing our own.  Have we become our own murdering marauding white sheets?

Open your eyes:  at the same time over 20,000 young A-A are dying at the hands of other A-As in reckless gun violence every year, Technology companies import 50,00 foreign workers as engineers, software designers, security experts, analyst, etc.  You are killing each other for stupid reasons in the form of mental slavery fed to you over the air waves and electronic media.  Open your eyes and see what you are doing to our community.  Then stop it because it is tantamount to engaging in self-inflicted wickedness and so egregious that it is plain stupid.

Check yourself, let go of the anger towards your fellow A-A and your willingness to engage in  hostile words and actions against them.  You cannot control someone's mouth only your own.

Someone else's destruction provides a very unstable foundation for your construction.  Besides, cause and effect are absolute.  The causes you make are like a boomerang in your life, and the lives of members of your family and by extension your community.

For example, it is against your basic humanity and dignity to stand around and watch, or participate in physical altercations between fellow A-As.  Not to mention the barbaric mentality you display when you share such activities in the Cyber world.  Sometimes the karmic retribution may not appear until a succeeding generation but appear it will, and the retribution will ensue.  "What ye sow..."

8.      Since the 1860's, A-A men and boys have been trolled day and night.  Use this fact as the catalyst to reenergize and renew your unwavering determination to be the master of your own fate.   It is a motivator to strengthen your good qualities and polish your character daily.  Develop genuineness and booster your courage by confidently taking on life's struggles and inevitable challenges.  Use obstacles as your greatest motivator and opportunity to polish your fortitude. *When life circumstances become a lemon, make lemonade, and feel refreshed.*

9.      Analyze this.  Less than 2% of the great, super great and most skilled high school basketball and football players ever wear a Pro uniform or play Professional ball.  During your foundational

> **These young guys are playing checkers.  I am out there playing chess.**
>
> **Everything negative including pressure and challenges is all an opportunity for me to rise.**
>
> **Kobe Bryant  24**

years in school, such a dream of being a professional athlete as a career choice is admirable, but it is imperative that you choose study and serious academic mastery as your first choice in preparation to afford yourself multiple career choices instead of attending school only to play sports and ending up with broken dreams with no way out of a life to be lived with regret.  During the years of your youth, you must take seriously the foundation you lay on which you will have to stand as an adult to positively sustain yourself and possibly a family.   Youth Prepare Yourself (YPY).

10.	Remember you are accountable to tenaciously accept the torch from your parents and continue our customs and traditions, to progress even further than their achievements.  To always seek wisdom from the sages and griots.

11.	**Before you decide on something, always examine alternatives and their possible long and short-term consequences.**

12.	Youthful A-A men, there is no human mental and physical prowess greater than yours in this Universe. When it comes to mental and physical prowess, know and embrace this truth " you are the Alpha and the Omega." Believe in your Divine gifts. You, my awesome brothers, must cease and desist all efforts by others to control your psychic to where you kill and harm each other, thus marginalizing our people.  I am confident that you will proudly and effectively rise and take back your mental health.



13.	The underlying truth is you as an A-A male is feared for your physical prowess and your mental sagacity.  You are always under attack to keep you off balance and from realizing or capitalizing on your natural mental and physical prowess.  The biggest fears of all is your ceasing to turn on your own brothers, uniting and moving back to focusing on the greatness of our ancestors, because you will be unstoppable.  It is fear of you that keep our communities under attack, our civil, voting, and Constitutional rights under attack.  The upside is to stop engaging in mental slavery and helping with our own destruction.

14.     Know that when you are mean and wicked to others, participating in bulling, or standing around watching and witnessing violence, you are defiling your humanity and insulting our ancestors.  During the wicked time when hangings were being carried out, often the EA community would come out to watch and witness the murder of our ancestors.  Not to mention the barbaric mentality you display when you share such activities in the Cyber world.   Our humanity demands that we help not hurt.  Check yourself.

15.     Around age 12, you will begin preparing for your ***Rite of Passage Gathering*** to be held shortly after you turn 14.

**What an elder see's while sitting,**

**a youth cannot see while standing**.

African Proverb.

<u>**A-A Youth**</u>

<u>**Some Careers that Pay Well**</u>

*Coding, Information Technology (IT),  Cyber Security, Cyber Warfare*

*Gig Economy, Alternative Currencies, Esports*

*Artificial Intelligence (AI), Robotics,  Engineering*

*Finance/Venture Capitalism.*

*Science, Technology, Engineering,  Math*

*Music,  Art, Animation, Global Economics, Law*

*Astrophysics, Quantum Physics*

*Government, Civics, Capitalism, Economics*

*Medicine, Research,  Nursing, Gene Therapy*

*Space Exploration, Interplanetary Transport*

*Universal Transportation*

*Professional Sports*

*Environmental Science,  Environmental  Studies, Oceanography*

*Pedagogy*

*Customer Relations Management (CRM)*

*Green Space Design, Hybrid Landscaping, Urban Design*

*Biotechnology*          *( add a few more below)*

______________________________________________

______________________________________________

Female youth of A-A descent are sagacious, unafraid, mentally astute, and determined group of multitaskers.   The ancestors extended you endless fortitude, invincibility, grace, and courage.

**A-A Female Youth: Know these things:**

1. A-A girls are graceful, dignified, respect themselves, have self-worth and gladly embrace their femininity.  They take precious care of their bodies through proper diet, strength training, meditation, and yoga.  They know to steer clear of toxins: certain people, environments, mind-altering substances, and to never engage in negative activities.

   *Katherine Gobal Johnson* **accurately calculated the trajectory to get John Glenn to the moon and back safely.**
   *Sarah Elisabeth Goode*, **Inventor**
   *Gabrella Wilson*, **Child Music Prodigy**
   *Althea Gipson*
   *Serena Williams,  Ginger Howard*
   *Emma "Ginger" Smock,*
   *Alice Parker, Jackie Venson,*
   *Lt. General Nadia West,*
   *Mariah Stackhouse, Sadena Parks*
   *Florence Price, Cheynne Woods*
   *Dr. Patricia E. Bath*

2. Youth is the time of academic preparation, foundation laying, character, and emotional development.  Most of all it is the time of listening and learning from your parents and elders.  It is when you learn how to treat, appreciate, and extend kindness to others.

3. Youth is the time when the foundations of life are modeled and taught to you.  Often referred to as the five Ss: Self-reliance, self-respect, self-determination, self-motivation, and self-sustainability.

A-A young female is careful and selective in all aspects of her life.  She seeks her purpose and embraces it with gusto.  She knows that it is fruitless to waste time gossiping, bulling others, responding to gossip, or participating in this blatantly negative energy creation.

Routinely, A-A girls learn from their mother's and grandmother's social etiquette and common courtesies, respect for their bodies and dressing with an abundance of decency.

4.  She knows that her body is her temple.  It must be given the upmost of respect by herself and everyone else.  She must never allow herself to be abused, disrespect,  or misused in any way.
5.  She keeps a daily dowry, documenting her daily thoughts and experiences.
6.  This is your time for academic preparation across reading, civics, math, science, engineering, technology, economics, history, music, languages, and art.

7.  A-A girls always dress with a modicum of decency and class, never revealing private body parts and a hemline on or below the knee.

8.  Remember you are accountable to tenaciously accept the torch from your parents , continue our customs and traditions, and to progress even further than their achievements.  Always seek wisdom from the sages and griots.

9.  Around age 12, you will begin to prepare for your upcoming Melanin *Cotillion* at age  14.

10 .  Check yourself and let go of the anger towards your fellow A-As and your willingness to engage in  hostile words and actions against them.  You cannot control

someone's mouth only your own. Someone else's destruction provides a very unstable

foundation for your construction. Besides, cause and effect are absolute. For example, it is against our basic humanity and dignity to stand around and watch, or participate in physical altercations between fellow A-As.  Not to mention the barbaric mentality you display when you share such activities in the Cyber world.   Our humanity demands that we help not hurt.

Catana Starks, Simone Biles,  Cabby Douglas, Althea Gibson, Jackie Joyner Kersee, Sidney Leroux,  Ora Washington, Alice Coachman, Louise Stokes, Tidye Pickett, Florence Griffith Joyner, Allyson Felix, Marion Jones,  Lisa Leslie, Sanya Richards-Ross, Sheryl Swoops, Brianna Scurry, Venus Williams, Cheryl Miller, Cynthia  Cooper, Chrystal Dunn, Carmelita Jeter, Jessica McDonald, Shasta Averyhardt

*Your favorites*: ___________________________

___________________________________________

# Chapter 10

## With Our Eyes Opened

## Living Our Inherited Greatness

With our eyes opened, we acknowledge that we are engaged in hand to hand combat for our very survival.  With opened eyes, we stand and proclaim ENOUGH. NO MORE.  We choose to erase the residual muck left by the Stockholm Syndrome and cease behaving contrary to our own interest.  We recognize it is imperative that we stop aiding oppression with some of our behaviors and willingly destroying our own people. Often, we make such severe negative causes that we undermined ourselves and attract into our communities' multitudes of negativity and destruction, due to karmic retribution.  The Law of Cause and Effect is absolute.  Going forward, we choose to make better causes (choices) and act and react in concert with living our inherited greatness across all aspects of our community.

To live our greatness, we must first turn inward and correct our own house.  While negative life tendencies are inherent in the Universe and encountered by all, we refuse to continue to be victims and confirm instead to be our best selves. Only we can make the necessary internal structural changes to form a solid foundation on which generations now and future generations can stand.  The time is now.  The person is you.  Lasting change begins from within you. It always starts with the "man in the mirror." Surely only we can save ourselves, our culture, our dignity, our children, our communities, protect and ensure our Constitutional Rights.  It cannot be overstated;  such a monumental change requires individual human revolution in the form of self-transformation and self-accountability.

To live our greatness as a community and culture, we will produce <u>more</u> strong, confident, economically productive, and real men with a sense of positive self-worth who supports their wife and children and is Civic participating.  We need more strong real men who are Central Figures in the home, who stand tall in the home. Think back when you have walked into a bank and an A-A couple is at the desk or in the office transacting business with a banker.  Most times, the A-A woman is doing the talking with the man sitting there looking submissive.  I have observed the same at School Parent Nights.  In many instances if the father comes with the mother, the mother leads the conversation with the teacher or principal. You will rarely see this with other cultures because the man is accountable and confident to speak for the family and examples his role as the Central Figure for his children.  Many more genuine A-A men must raise their heads, stand tall and take their place in the family and community.

**1st A-A Public High School was Paul Lawrence Dunbar High School in Washington D.C. in 1870.**

**The pedagogy work of Marva Collins**

To live our greatness as a community **we must help raise the child to self-sustaining adulthood.**  We must support our youth without haste.  Children are like the corn kernels on a cobb.  The cobb is the parents and the community.  We must keep the children close, safe, studying academics across disciplines including languages, music, creative thinking, collaboration, problem solving, and learning our traditions and history.  We must become accountable for A-A values and positive self-worth being passed on to our children.  Know that education/pedagogy is a treasure that can never be stolen from them.  It is a treasure that endures for a lifetime. Education is the greatest wealth our children can attain in this world.  It is the wealth that will give them satisfaction, a sense of accomplishment, save them from destruction, and prepare them to compete as global citizens. It is the underpinning of productive citizenship and a life well lived.  It is time for us to return to Parenting for self-reliance and self-sustainability using education and faith as the cornerstones. Let us be good stewards maintaining wholesome family units where children thrive into self-respecting adults. This is our most important task.  Again, we must be accountable for raising our children to be respectful, descent, and productive Civic participating citizens and great neighbors.

We live our greatness when adults model for our youth constructive, unified, respectful examples of adult interactions. Never exposing them to loud, abrasive, foul mouth, undignified, rude, backbiting, and backstabbing conflicts. We dare not expose our youth to poor examples of how to navigate conflicts.  A-A adults are supposed to set examples for children to emulate.  What are we thinking?  We should think carefully before deliberately interjecting a bunch of negative, loudmouth, repugnant, toxic nonsense as pretense entertainment while our boys are being shot down in the streets and many of our children are exposed to toxins in their drinking water and subjected to deficient public education.  Get a grip my people and become accountable to model constructive, respectful adult interactions premised on these being teachable moments.

We live our greatness by carefully choosing what and how we allow ourselves to be portrayed in the public sphere.  Considering other cultures are not subjected to relentless injustices, attempts at marginalization, or outright destruction as are we, they can afford to display themselves in loud, rude inner fighting groups, calling each other belittling names, and generally modeling bad behaviors.  We, on the other hand, cannot afford to feed this type of negative messaging to our youth and the world especially projecting it as acceptable behavior. Let us not forget our history of the forced skinning and grinning as entertainment for the CI. Excessive preferences for clowning and joking around in our communities can suggest to our youth that a lack of seriousness is a meaningful way to use precious formative years. Many High Schools in communities of color are riddled with the propensity of students to clown and joke around instead of embracing serious academic study.  The truth is the joke is on us.  It is time to get serious.

To live our greatness, our men and boys must stop killing each other without reservation, hesitation, or indifference.   It is depraved to shoot down your own brothers.  **Ask yourselves, why are you doing the bidding of self-hate, self-destruction and performing as a thoughtless puppet for those out to marginalize and destroy us?**  And for those of us guilty of implanting this seed and perpetuating and glorifying animosity between our young brethren while continued to advance financially by nourishing and glorifying it for five decades over the airways, byways, social media, through encouraged adversarial affiliations, glorified confrontational behaviors and actions thereby leading your own brothers to slaughter or an early grave, you need to check your self-hatred and mental slavery. You are wrong.  Ask yourself, why am I writing or speaking angry threating inciteful words to share among my own people?  What am I thinking?  Now that many have made money

> **What is happening on the outside in your life, merely reflects what is occurring on the inside of you.  The Universe bends to your life condition.**
>
> **The same is true in our Communities.**

teaching our boys to kill, ***try teaching them how to live, unify, and support each other.***  Teach them *how* to uplift and support their communities instead of showering brother on brother violence, grief, destruction, and leaving fatherless children  who are often saddled with unnecessary barriers to learning including adverse living environments.

**Many of you who have ridden this wave of vocalizing inner community animosity and thereby fostering violence against each other and senseless deaths, are now trying to shelter your own children from the morass you have helped create.**  Think about all the dead boys, men, grieving families, fatherless children, and the negative impact on our voting potential going forward.  I ask you to remember **"what ye sow……."**  Did you ever wonder why the major labels were so  agreeable early on to get behind our peddling self-hate and inter-community violence?  Do you think if these were EAs feeding poison to their own youth, the labels would have so eagerly stepped up and bank rolled it?  **Think, my people, think.**  We can embrace wonderful music without the anger, self-hate, threats, aggression, and highlighted self-destruction of our own men and boys and by extension women and girls.

If you are a part of any industry that produces entertainment to our community that teaches poor character, hatred and violence against your brethren, backbiting, backstabbing, loud, rude, often promiscuous behaviors and lude dress, **you need to stop right now.  You have been weaponized against your own people.**  Most cultures pride themselves on being shown in their best light around the world.  Sharing the many positive aspects of their culture.  Many of us lead our people and especially our young to self-destruction.  <u>Today, the manifestation of mental slavery is at work.</u>

We live our greatness by taking responsibility for our community. There will always be excuses and enough blame to fill the Universe, but we must take responsibility for our community. In the end, we are responsible for what is happening in our Communities today.  Yes, many of the bad things are being assisted or orchestrated by outsiders such as the easy access to handguns, but ultimately, we are still responsible because we are allowing it to happen here in the 21st century and thereafter.

We live our greatness when we finally shake off the mental shackles of a crab mentality, unite, build and support our economic infrastructure like our ancestors envisioned and ultimately accomplished on Black Wall Street in Tulsa, Oklahoma before it was deliberately targeted and wickedly destroyed at the hands of the same hate that is showing its face so egregiously today.  With dauntless courage and a powerful inner determination, we will protect our A-A Communities with our very lives.

> **A. G. Gaston of Birmingham**
> **The Greenwood District-Black Wall Street**

We live our greatness by teaching our history at home every day, and *reinforce it* on major holidays especially Kwanzaa, MLK Holiday, Memorial Day for those that made the ultimate sacrifice from the Revolutionary War and every war thereafter; Juneteenth- A-A History Month, the Festival of Lights in early October, and Family Reunions.  I propose we move A-A History Month to June and celebrate the month with Juneteenth commemorating the 1865 notification to A-A in bondage in Texas that the Emancipation of 1863 had granted their freedom.  This is the true end of *Dejure Slavery.* *Historically February was chosen to celebrate A-A History because Abraham Lincoln and Fredrick Douglas were both born in February.  But the truth is President Lincoln was willing to allow slavery*

> **Samuel Cornish & John Russwurm,** *Freedom Journal*
> **Barry Gordy,** *Motown*
> **John H. Johnson,** *Jet & Ebony*
> **Earl Graves, Sr.,** *Black Enterprise Magazine*
> **Essence Communications Inc**.
> **Nearest Green, Distiller**

*to continue in the South in the form of allowing the South to continue with its <u>Peculiar Institution</u> but insisted slavery could not be extended beyond the South.* He signed the Emancipation Proclamation as a vehicle to punish the succeeding states. If you study, you will realize the Emancipation Proclamation initially freed those held in bondage in the Southern States and not, for example, even in the District of Columbia. Had the Southern States agreed to contain human bondage within its borders, there may not have been a Civil War and slavery would have remained in the South unabated except for overseas importation until the slaves would have risen-up and taken their freedom.

> **C.L.R. James**
> **Mayor Maynard Jackson, Jr. of Atlanta**
>
> ***The Black Jacobins***
>
> ***Matthew Whitaker, Jazz Pianist***
>
> ***The Negro League***

We must **teach** our true history in our homes, community centers, fellowship halls, and town squares. It is time to stop blaming others for our omissions from the books and teach our own. It is time to write the history books that factually and extensively present the history of the A-A people. We must engage in deliberate study.

To live our greatness, we now open our eyes to the redemptive knowledge taught by our ancestors that sustainable agriculture is our way. We must take control of what we are eating and feeding to our children. Is it true that a certain baby formula is overwhelmingly prescribed to A-A babies? Watch it...

> **Henry Louis Gates, Jr.**
> ***Life Upon These Shores.***
> **John Hope Franklin**
> **Carter G. Woodson**
> **Dorothy Height**
> **Andrew Young**, ***UN Ambassador, Civil Rights Icon, former Mayor of Atlanta, Entrepreneur***

To live our greatness, we must recognize destruction from within our families and communities is the most dangerous. The traps are laid, so let us be mindful and never overstimulate our minds and bodies with toxins such as excessive drugs, alcohol, food apartheid, and interpersonal conflicts that lead to death.  Excessive eating clogs the body and the mind.  Remember to FAST a minimum of several times during a 12-moon cycle.

Now that our Eyes Are Opened expect more great things and to do more great things as a people.  Different experiences may arise that challenge your vision, but still expect greatness, no matter what shape life has taken on in the present moment, expect greatness.  Greatness revolves

Rev. Dr. Martin Luther King, Jr.

*"If you can't fly then run, if you can't run then walk, if you can't walk, then crawl, but whatever you do, you must keep moving forward."*

*Nelson Mandela "**Who are you not to be great**"*

around one's frame of mind.  When you allow your mind to fly with eagles, good things will manifest because the shadow follows the body.  Everything revolves around the way you think followed by your actions.  So, with a positive, enduring, and courageous mindset, continue to expect greatness and act accordingly and it shall be ours.  We will achieve unity of purpose and work together for common goals. With dauntless courage and a powerful inner determination, we will protect our A-A Community with our lives.

Again, we see you clearly along with the wickedness deliberately and methodically done to our people, and we wholeheartedly admit the residual harm we have done to ourselves. It ends now.  We are no longer residual carriers of the Stockholm Syndrome and will not act and react at our own detriment. NO MORE.  We are not afraid.  WE DO NOT SCRATCH IF WE DO NOT ITCH, AND WE DO NOT LAUGH UNESS WE DEEM SOMETHING TO BE FUNNY. Through it all today, we the A-A people proudly stand as survivors.  It is a testament to our mental and physical prowess, and unwavering life force to have survived.  To this day,  surviving such extreme evil attest to our invincibility, our fortitude, and most of all our ancestors watching over us for we are still standing.

Each of us must determine to never participate in the on-going ploy to discredit, demean, destroy, and marginalize our people.   Instead we will live our greatness by achieving unity of purpose and work together (ujamaa) for common goals. Recognizing the intense and unrelenting struggle ahead as PNW strategies are hurled at us relentlessly.   A self-sustaining civic participating future awaits us.

Further, if those of us living today would free our minds and stop self-destructing, newborns will not inherit the identity problems.  We can correct this in our lifetime.   "Imagine that …" Parents are role models in families and in the community.  If the child grows up seeing the father or parents go off to work every day, work and supporting the family will be what the child aspires to accomplish.  The same with reading, study, lifelong learning, and voting.

We have move away from skin colon and onto culture. We no longer see or describe ourselves as a color but an awesome culture with traditions and ancestral greatness.  We cease referring anything related to us with the color black for we are so much more than a color. We are African-Americans.

Ultimate sacrifice: **Addie Mae Collins, Cynthia Wesley, Carol Robertson, and Carol Denise McNair**

**The fifth victim who was severely injured: Sarah Collins**

Now that we are clear and conscious of the embedded transmitted tendencies , we can effectively counter them.   When you find yourself leaning towards mentally slavery tendencies,(MSI) step back from the abyss, regroup mentally, forgive yourself and replace the MSI tendency with a positive cultural norm.

I say to my people: just think, having endured the deliberately applied physical and mental sufferings, wicked, covert, and overt actions, and encouragements to self-defeatism, **we are still standing.** Though deliberately and relentlessly oppressed for many generations, we are still standing and now choose to remove evil from our psychic, and stand on the foundation of grit, invincibility, and fortitude inherited from our ancestors. We are resilient and descend from a mighty people. Nothing has completely broken us. For (we) could not and will not be broken. History will document "a people, who after 246 years of the most wretched physical, and mental abuse, racial and sexual terrorism could not be broken." History will refer to us as a people who finally removed the psycho drama, shed the vestiges of the Stockholm Syndrome, proclaimed their Divine Righteous Place and embraced the 5 Ss throughout their existence: Self-worth, Self-respect, Self-determination, Self-sustainability, and Service.

"NO MORE" is our Battle Cry. We say to EAs, we will never forget the disdain with which you interacted with us along our JOURNEY here in America, but we see it as our impetus, it underscores our determination and unwavering will to become the great people for which we are ordained and destined. This has become our Zeitgeist. My people, I wish each of you well on this fantastic life journey.

Congratulations as we shake off the last vestiges from The Wicked Time and claim our righteous place and refocus our energies on possibilities. Remember the purpose of this life is to achieve happiness by living our purpose, parenting capable children to self-sustaining adulthood, and extend help to those in distress.

**A-As do your part** and spread the word about the Truth in this book.  It must be read, said, and retold over the generations to come as we navigate this Babylon. The time is now, and the responsible person is you.  Again, lasting change begins from within. It always starts with the "man in the mirror." Surely only WE can save ourselves, our culture, our dignity, our children, our communities, and protect and ensure our Constitutional Rights.  This charge requires our human revolution in the form of individual self-transformation and self-accountability.

As a people,  we must always embrace and **embody the dignity, classiness, and professionalism** that was the bedrock of **Motown**. Embodying  quality character traits and classiness in our daily lives, the entertainment industry, and the general  marketplace is critical. As entertainers and as individuals, what you show people around the world is how they will see us.  How they **will judge our culture and view our children**.

*Thanks Mr. Barry Gordy.*

*You understood the importance of Positive Messaging*

# Chapter 11

## A-A Political Discourse

## We Will Determine for Ourselves

**Political Parties**

Definition: *"To rule the nation if they could but see it dammed if others should."*  The Constitution of the United States of America does not provide for, call for, or encourage Political Parties.  The Bill of Rights does not call for Political Parties and none of the existing twenty-eight amendments establish political parties. We should consider leaving the two-party system and voting as Independents meaning you are free to support any candidate you deem the right fit for the job.   My father Joel Hamilton told me repeatedly growing up, "the Democratic Party or Republican

> Angela Davis
>
> **I am no longer accepting the things I cannot change.  I am changing the things that I cannot accept**

Party, as far as we are concerned, there is not a dimes' worth of difference. For the A-A, the outcome is the same.  One Party stabs you in the back, the other Party stabs you in the chest. Either way you are dead...."  Again, the Constitution does not establish Political Parties.  The "Founding Fathers" saw fit to write seven detailed articles and shortly after ratification, added ten amendments.  Nowhere in this auspicious document do these one hundred men mention political parties being the foundation on which the national government is to organize and run.

There are no Amendments to the Constitution of the United States authorizing Political Parties, thus they should be done away with for the redemption of the nation.  If left alone, they will destroy the nation from within.  The first President of the United States, George Washington, warned us against establishing political parties and joining foreign treaties.  The two major Political Parties (Republican and Democrat) have become a hegemon with a chokehold on the nation.

A person willing or wishing to serve in government should be able to declare and run for office simply as a CITIZEN having met the requirements of age, citizenship etc.  Ballots should simply list the name of the candidates.  We should not vote as liberal, conservative, progressive, libertarian, left, or right wing.  We should simply vote for the right person for the job on behalf of our people.  The Congress of the United States of American should operate as outlined in the Constitution and not based on Majority and Minority Party nonsense.  Further, this unconstitutional juggernaut has taken control of State Houses, County and City Houses, and sometimes I think even any Outhouses that are left.

Ask yourself: Does it make sense that the Constitutionally established (Article 1) Congress is currently organized around a political party concept that is non-constitutional.  Most of our government is operating outside of the Constitution.  I say, this is destructive for the Country.  It leads to gridlock, prevents many true public servants from coming forward, relegates the integrity of our political system to money and those with money,

> *"Our visit to this planet is short, so we should use our time meaningfully, which we  can do by helping others whenever possible. And if we cannot help others, at least we should **try not** to create pain and suffering for them."*
>
> *His Holiness the 14th Dalai Lama*

and for the most part, prevents honesty and best outcomes from being the basis for decision making.  It infuses a climate of incivility, mistrust, and government that does not serve with an underlying mission of best outcomes for all people  especially in the Tax Code which is written to allow the wealthy  to use loopholes to avoid paying while the middle  class is severely taxed and cruelly held accountable.

Those elected to serve in the Senate or House of Representatives should report to Washington D.C. on January 5th and depart no later than March 30th spending limited time in Washington D.D.  Their agenda:  balance the budget, provide for the National Defense which includes the Military and Public Education, Security; promote the general welfare of the country which includes the environment, infrastructure, retirees, and health care.  Any necessary new or revised laws are written or modified and enacted on during this period.  The President of the United States can convene one Emergency Session of Congress within a 12-month period lasting no more than 14 days in duration.  Can you imagine the amount of paper (trees), ink, hours, we have devoured since 1900 writing bills?  Many overlaps or contradict bills from previous years. Every Congress writes more and more lengthy bills.  Storing this stuff alone must be a nightmare.

Historically many, once mighty, empires have been destroyed from within usually attributed to internal decay.  Political Parties are the catalyst for the destruction of the United States.  The electorate is not being served, big money donors are in control of our statehouses and national government.  To remove them and get back to Articles 1 and 2 of the Constitution will, more than likely, require a Constitutional Amendment to dismantle Political Parties.

## Public Education

Did you know that the initial framers of the Constitution did not view public education as a national right or need?   This is the reason Public Education is left up to the States.  When in fact, since quality educated people are the first and most important defense strategy of any country, Public Education should become a branch of the Department of Defense.  It would change the entire structure and bring the necessary focus, discipline, consistency, quality learning and training necessary to compete in this Universe being driven by ever advancing technology.

Fifty states with 50 different curriculums will not bold well for such a universal marketplace where other countries pride themselves on consistency and quality preparation. So, we hire immigrants to fill highly technical jobs then complain about immigrants and spies. We fill our higher learning institutions with foreign students.  Why are we not aggressively educating our own citizens first?  Oh, because we would need to finally extend quality Public Education across all communities to prepare students based on equity, and cease deliberately under-educating certain communities.

The grossly unsatisfactory almost criminal performance of the Department of Education and Congress especially as it relates to providing substandard public schools in marginalized communities is disgraceful. Especially considering the billions and billions spend on Consultants, textbook companies, and let us not forget the suppliers of poor-quality food.  We should be aware of who can oversee the writing of history textbooks used in Public Schools as they are subject to gross omissions, slanted truths, and narrow interpretations.  History textbooks are weak on history and in the case of World History, steadfastly focuses on European history when

Africa existed for millions of years before the CI invaded. That is the primary reason we must teach our own history in our homes, recreation centers, and places of worship.

## Develop Economic Infrastructures Within Our Communities

Our ancestors showed us the way to self-sustainability.  There was a Greenwood District referred to as "Black Wall Street," a self-sufficient City  in Tulsa Oklahoma with its on banks and  other businesses owned and supported by A-As, complete with home ownership and an education system.  It was burned to the ground and many of its inhabitants murdered by a cowardly CI mob roaming the sheets.  This sent a chill across any other A-A self-sustaining thinkers about becoming self-supporting and self-sustaining.   Its message was "remain a defacto slave or be destroyed." We were Free but not free.  We must use the example left to us and become the entrepreneurs, community protectors, and supporters of each other.

**Celebrating A-A History**.  I propose we change the celebration to June to coincide with the especially important Emancipation celebration of Juneteenth.  February was initially chosen because it is the birthday month of Abraham Lincoln and Frederick Douglas.  While being against slavery on a personal level, it must be pointed out that before the firing on Fort Sumter, Abraham Lincoln was willing to allow the South to keep its Peculiar Institution within the Southern borders.   He wrote and signed the Emancipation Proclamation to punish the states that had committed treason against the United States.

Besides, in June , the children are out of school and can study their A-A history extensively and participate in parades. Community, family, and faith celebrations can be numerous.  We should anchor our history month celebration to the DeJure End of Slavery which occurred in Galveston Texas in 1865.

**Amendments, Referendums, and Ballot Initiatives.**  We must judiciously examine and analyze amendments, referendums, and initiatives.  These can become law.  Never fluff over amendments.  We must understand them and their underlying impact on our people and communities.  Always  cast your vote.

<u>Frederick Douglas, Circa 1880 on the 4<sup>th</sup> of July holiday</u>.  "What, to the American slave, is your 4<sup>th</sup> of July? "I answer a day that reveals to him, more than all other days in the year, the gross injustice and cruelty to which he is the constant victim.  To him, your celebration is a sham; your boasted liberty, an unholy license; your national greatness, selling vanity; your denunciation of tyrants, a brass fronted imprudence; your shouts of liberty and equality, hollow mockery; your prayers and hymns, your sermons and thanksgivings, will all your religious parade and solemnity are, to Him, mere bombast, fraud, deception, impiety, and hypocrisy – a thin veil to cover up crimes which would disgrace a nation of savages."  "There is not a nation on earth guilty of practices more shocking and bloodier than are the people of the United States, at this very hour."

> **We must learn languages**. Nelson Mandela said, "if you talk to a man in a language he understands, that goes to his head.  If you talk to him in his language, that goes to his heart."  **We should start with proper English , Spanish, then Chinese , and Arabic variations.**

Why not introduce our children to different languages at an early age when mastery is much easier.

Sovereign Nations :  a sovereign nation, like the United States, France, England, etc. has the right to develop nuclear technology, even though we wish none did.  But do they have the right to dictate to another sovereign nation what it can or cannot do within its sovereign borders?  What gives one nation the authority to tell another nation what it can or cannot do?  Military Power and might does not make right.   It makes for Imperialism, bullying,  self-righteousness, and  a "do as I say and not as I do application of foreign policy."  Wicked character traits.

Our Young A-A boys and girls and  are being exploited for their athletic prowess to earn billions and billions for Athletic Programs whose schools have minimal A-A enrollment and little to no significant economic outreach to A-A communities.  Exploiting labor and making billions of dollars under the guise of "they are getting a free education." Have you noticed that we do not see an annual mandated accounting of the so called "top 25 schools" and their performances in graduating our athletes?  Look back over the last 30 years.

% of A-A athletes in football and basketball who graduated in 4 years

% of A-A athletes in football and basketball who graduated in 5 years

% of A-A athletes in football and basketball who turned pro early

% of A-A athletes in football and basketball who received a pro contract

% of A-A athletes in football and basketball who played out their eligibility and did not graduate.  Where did they end up?

% of A-A athletes in football and basketball graduating in various fields of study.

These athletes dutifully glorify the stadium or arena while exposing themselves to lifelong mental and physical injuries without a hint of compensation.  This is unjust. They do their job as Gladiators for the arena generating billions for others. The sharing of revenue is easy to fix and the human, decent and fair thing to do.  For example, Schools can be mandated to contribute 2%

of their Athletic Program's **gross** earnings to a collective escrow account.  Upon graduation or separation, players will receive a bonus payment.  Financial gurus can establish a viable framework.  Suffice it to say, something needs to be done about the Twenty First Century  Style of Stolen Labor. Our people make up an exceedingly small percentage of enrollment in these schools.  The billions our young athletes earn for these schools are not going to educate our people or uplift our communities in any significant way.

We support our young athletes who play their hearts out and wish them well and encourage them to make sure they graduate with a degree that can open doors to a self-sustaining lifestyle if a pro team does not come calling.  Consider the  degree as your spare tire.  Every car needs a spare tire.  In case you do not "go pro" or become injured early on, you can fall back and ride on your spare tire.

### Read, Read, Read a variety of inputs

**Books: For example, Ta-Nehisi Coates**:

> Black Panther, Captain America,

> Between the World and Me,  The Water Dancer and more...

**The Constitution of the United States of America**

**Your State Constitution**

**Your Board of Education Policy(ies), Your local County & City Ordinances**

**Your local Media, National Credible Media, World Media**

# Example of Moving to Community Self-sufficiency

## The Black Panther Party for Self-Defense

The Black Panthers for Self-Defense were great champions.  They defended not turning the other cheek  especially when violence is executed against the community  and embraced Malcom's "by any means necessary" to defend the community.  They emphasized getting our people elected to office by encouraging voting in every election. They taught self-help, fed the hungry, provided access to healthcare, stood up and fought for justice for those in our communities being subjected to injustice and frame-ups, led voter registrations initiatives, and chose to stand like men to defend the community from police brutality, and other forms of attack.  They formed armed citizen patrols. They also stood for anti-imperialism, for self-sustainability,  and  productivity in the community.



Most of them were unjustly murdered or jailed to shut down any A-A attempt at self-improvement and self-empowerment. They would be targeted with counterintelligence, paid infiltrators, and snitches,  then jailed on trumped up charges, or murdered by the ___ ___ ___. Destroyed for standing up and trying to do a good thing: Huey Newton, Bobby Seal, Elbert Howard, Stockley Carmichael, Kathleen Cleaver, H. Rap Brown, Charlotte O'Neal, Fredricka Newton, and Eldridge Cleaver,  and  many others, we say thank you for seeing the true life-line path of <u>self-sustainability</u> and trying to move our community in that direction.

# The Nature of Money or Currency

Some say money buys everything.  <u>Not true</u>.  It cannot extend your life when your time is up.  It can exacerbate greed, selfishness, and foolishness in people's hearts.  The fact that no one gets out of this universe alive should humble us.  Neither love, hate, money, or skin pigmentation will keep us alive forever.  This means to generate much barter is important but not at the expense of your dignity, or that inflicts harm on your people or community .

## Does Time Exist?

The Universe is always now. There is really no such thing as **time** in the Universe.  Humans invented *time* to mark their **birth, old age, sickness, and death**.  The date and time are always <u>now.</u>  We age on our way to reckoning with a destined exit, but  does time does really exist?  Think about it

## Question

Looking back from today did the Talented Tenth Fail?  Was Booker T. Washington Right?

Flat Top Personal Income Tax of 10%.   Persons making less than $25,000 annually and anyone over 70 years of age should not be taxed.  Every person, business, or entity making over $25,000 should pay.  No loopholes for the wealthy, no passes, no waivers, and no state income taxes. The Constitution provides for the collection of Federal Income Taxes in the Sixteenth Amendment but did not mention State Income taxes, although it does leave items not mentioned

Dick Gregory

**I wouldn't  mind paying taxes if I knew they were going to a friendly country**

up to the States.  The Federal government should dispense monies back to the states based on population size after providing for the national defense including homeland security and promoting the general welfare of the country (retirement, infrastructure, public education, environment, unemployment).   Look at this semi-flat example:

| Income     Range | Pay this Amount |
| --- | --- |
| 0       - 25,000 | No taxes.  No taxing people over 70 years of age |
| 26,000 - 30,000 | 1% |
| 31,000- 35,000 | 1% |
| 36,000 - 40,000 | 2% |
| 41,000 - 45,000 | 3% |
| 46,000 - 50,000 | 4% |
| 51,000 - 60,000 | 5% |
| 61,000 - 70,000 | 7% |
| 75,000 - 80,000 | 9% |
| 80,000 and above | 10% |

Imagine, taking only five minutes to complete your taxes.  It is critical we eliminate the middle-class crushing loophole tax system in place today that allows workarounds and exemptions for massive money earning entities and the top 5%,  but institutionally and systematically saddles the middle class with carrying the heavy burden of over taxation.  We should all stand-up for fairness and justice.  One way is a flat top tax rate not to exceed 10%  and applied on a graduated scale.  It should become an Amendment to the United States Constitution.

**Know the Laws:**  Study and know the Laws of the United States and their correct applications. Study, local, national, and even universal.  Know your rights.

**Protect Mother Earth:**  We must be vigilant in protecting Mother Earth.

---

## Question ????

### The Lost Tribe of Ethiopia

What happened to the Lost Tribe of Ethiopia?

What is our true history?????

---

## Flag

As African- Americans, perhaps we need to  adopt a flag that honors our ancestry .  Over the years,  we have used the  red, black, and green Pan-African Flag.   The Irish and Italian groups , along with many others, fly their flag  from time  to time.   We should come  up with our own and incorporate our  struggle, our  invincibility, and our  fortitude.  Perhaps this is a creative task for the Museum of African-American History at the Smithsonian in Washington, DC.

Here are some comments on colors.  Perhaps we need only choose three or four colors.  Perhaps you can  start thinking about it.

**Red.**  Red is the color of the life force blood shed by our ancestors during the African Holocaust and 400 years of Slavery in the Americas. It is our protective color and embodies our willpower, tenacity, invincibility, courage, and passion in all things especially the will to say and mean "NO More."  Red is our blood, strength, and determination.  Red is our laser focus on weeding out the wickedness amassed against us every day.  To which we say, 'No More, we see you."

**Blue.** Blue represents our wisdom and freeing ourselves from mental slavery including from the prolonged residual effects of brutal and sadistic human bondage. It acknowledges our trust of each other, our loyalty to one another, and our faith.  Blue calms the mind and engenders gratitude for the vast oceans and sky.

**Green.**  Green honors family: father, mother, children, grandparents; fertility, and procreation, as well as the community as a whole.  It acknowledges our oneness with nature, the environment, and procreation.  We embrace and value our forest and green spaces.

**Yellow :**  Celebrates the joy of life's potential or hope.  It reminds us to **meditate** daily, embrace humility though fasting often, and to remember extending kindness and  service to humanity is Divine.

**Purple:**      Divinity.  It also represents royalty  and grandeur.  It is the color of the crown chakra: the connection with spirituality.

**Black:**      If used to refer to skin color, then perhaps it does not belong on our flag.   What do you think?

Black is the absence of color because it absorbs all colors.  I would say that is pure. It is power and elegance.   "Black is required for all other colors to have depth and variation of hue https://www.bourncreative.com)."   Yet, even in many of our OWN religious settings, we elevate the color white, teaching our young that white is pure.   White is a combination of mixing primary colors or when we see all wavelengths of light and therefore cannot be pure.

Open your eyes to who wrote the description of colors and told the world that white is pure.  We must **choose for ourselves what is "pure"** and not teach our children to hate themselves.

## Symbols:

**The dollar signs:**  To represent 240 years of stolen labor, physical, mental, sexual abuse, and domestic terrorism; coupled with severe dehumanization at the hands of the Colonial Imperialists. One-dollar sign for every twenty years of human bondage and stolen labor.

**The raised fists**  Tells the world we are victims no more, we are not afraid, and we are fervently determined to build productive families and self-sustaining communities. It is a symbol of umoja, self-determination, self-sustainability, resistance, and self-defense of our communities and our people.

**What symbols do you suggest?**  _______________________________________

_______________________________________

# Chapter 12

## Challenge Yourself

Our innate fortitude has continued to propel us forward, no matter what,  henceforth, we A-A will make no excuses, no skinning and grinning, no killing our brethren, no peddling drugs to harm our people, no littering and destroying our neighborhoods, no absentee fathers making babies everywhere without caring for them, no uneducated children, no putting anything in our bodies that could control us, men will stand as men and take care of their families. No more Mental Slavery.  It ends today.  The family structure is the foundation of the A-A culture since the beginning.

We will maintain stable <u>Family Structures</u> as the norm.  Children need two parents whenever possible, nature deemed it so.  Parents are the role models for how to live productively, morally, and civically.  Parents are responsible for the formation of children's values and modes of behavior.

Many African American fathers and mothers do an effective job raising their children to be productive and civic minded citizens.  Sidney Poitier said, "the measure of a man is how well he takes care of his family." In the A-A community, the man is the head of the house and not the tail and supports his wife and children.

We will always be Kind and Just in our interactions with one another.  Never tattling to outsiders and backbiting.  We will aid each other in sickness and distress. we eat green leafy, red and or orange vegetables and nuts with every meal and eat minimally carbohydrates especially at major family feasts and celebrations.

Since 1901, the only legal slavery allowed in the United States is carried out as part of the Prison Industrial Complex.  We must avoid getting caught in this well woven net.  We must stop becoming fodder for the jails and cemetery.  Never engage in anything that will ultimately control you.

**We the <u>African-American</u> people** do not kowtow, ever.  **We do not laugh unless something is truly funny, we do not dance unless we hear music we favor, and we to not scratch unless we itch.**  The days of skinning and grinning in the hope of favor from the CI are over.  We will apply ourselves to our own development assiduously.

How we live each day, live each moment determines our future, the future of our families, and the future of our communities.  Confucius said, "worry not that no none knows of you; seek to be worth knowing."

**I have seen enough things to know that if you just keep on going,**

**if you turn the corner, the sun  will be shinning.**

**I always beat the sunup in the morning.  It is the secret  to why I**

**am double trouble (good trouble)      Rev. Al Sharpton**

<u>**Each of us must challenge ourselves**</u> **to become the change we want to see and experience in our communities.** We refuse to continue as  the best Consuming Group, but the poorest investors in our own communities.

Read and study this book with three persons you select and commit to help him/her become their best selves.

**This book is about choosing to act.  No more excuses.** Remember, if you light one candle in a dark room, the illumination is amazing.

**Having read this book, I challenge you to become active and set in motion a great wave of positive change in our communities, the likes of which the world has never seen.**

My people of the African American Diaspora: read this book carefully over and over, and then

share it with others in the African American Community, now and over the generations ...  Give it as a gift from your heart to others.  Now that your eyes have opened, and you know, that you know you can see clearly, and the fog has been lifted.  Teach the contents of this book to your children and their children, and your neighbors for all eternity.  **Do not put this book aside**.  Use it to help others.  ___What good is knowing if you fail to act.___  Use it to help at least three others.  Each one teaches one.

Allow **kind words** to emanate from your mouth and in your thoughts for yourself , your fellow A-As, and all you encounter.

"Say, I will be productive and courageous today.  I seek wisdom and courage in all aspects of my journey.  I will uplift my community today.   I will study today. And I will vote in every election."

Repeat these words individually and use them at Different Functions throughout the Community so our children will adopt them.

> *"Change will not come if we wait for some other person or if we wait for some other time.  We are the ones we have been waiting for.  We are the change that we seek."*
>
> *"Where we are met with cynicism and doubt and those who tell us that we cannot, we will respond with that timeless creed that sums up the spirit of our people:*
>
> ## *Yes, we can"*
>
> 44th President of the United States.
>
> **Barack  Hussein Obama**

Remember to financially support the National Museum of African American History and Culture at the Smithsonian in Washington, DC. the Equal Justice Initiative, National Memorial for Peace and Justice in Montgomery, Alabama, and our HBCU'S.

*This book ends  with my bow to <u>you my invincible people</u>*

**"The pure and Divine spirit in me acknowledges the pure and Divine spirit in each of you.  Go forth and do good works as you make the most of this journey called life."**

I implore you to **Aaliyah (to rise-up).**   Thank you for taking this journey with me.

**Read or recite the poem entitled "I See" on page 113 of this book.**

# The End

# Attachment

# African   Proverbs

**Africans on Africans**:  by nature, we are a sagacious people.  Sit with the sages and griots to listen often. They will tell you about your unlimited potential and your ability to do things that are extraordinary.  One thing they will share is the A-A people believe that the best place to find a helping hand is at the end of your own arm. Men of African descent are proud to be family men and stand for productive citizenship in their respective communities.    We cherish our children's futures.  We are people who create Value and believe wholeheartedly in Civic Engagement and Self-sustainability.

> **The number eight is endless, you cannot see where it begins or ends, and it symbolizes the continuousness of life**

We recognize the <u>innate four lower life conditions</u> operating in the Universe and by extension in the lives of individuals, communities, and even nations:  Hell, Anger, Self-destruction, and Apathy.  We must remain steadfast against the fundamental evils inherent in life that give rise to human suffering.

A  truly wise man will not be carried away by any of the eight winds:  prosperity, decline, disgrace, honor, praise, censure, suffering, and pleasure.  He is neither elated by prosperity nor grieved by decline.     … (Diashonin).

**African Proverbs:**

The fool speaks, the wise man listens.

The ears that do not listen to the wisdom of the elders, accompany the head when it is chopped off.  .

Do not tell your important secrets to your friend because your friend has other friends, as well.

By the time the fool has learned the game, the players have dispersed.

If you close your eyes to facts, you will learn through accidents.

In a moment of crisis, the wise build bridges, and the foolish builds dams.

Knowledge without wisdom is like water in the sand.  Wisdom does not come overnight.

If you are filled with pride, you have no room for wisdom.

If you have money at your disposal, every dog and goat will claim to be your friend  or
                     be related to you.

He who learns, teaches

It is not enough to have pride but no principles.

If you do not know where you are going, any road will take you there.

By crawling, a child learns to stand.

Bad friends will keep you from having good friends. .

Fools and weeds grow without rain. Yiddish.

Remain steadfast against the fundamental evils inherent in life that give rise to human suffering.  They are **greed, anger, and stupidity**.

No matter how long a log stays in the water, it does not become a crocodile

"When a fool goes shopping, the storekeeper rejoices.   Kristina Swarner."

It is difficult to receive if your hands are always closed.

**If poverty, injustice, and gross inequality persist here or in any part of Africa, none of us should rest.**

# Notes Page